serger ESSENTIALS

Master the Basics & Beyond!

Gail Patrice Yellen

Fons&Porter

CINCINNATI, OH

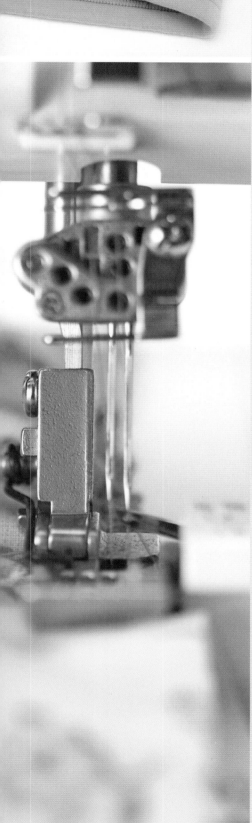

contents

foreword

BY NANCY ZIEMAN

WHEN PRESENTING SEMINARS, I generally ask the audience, "How many of you are serger owners?" My estimate is that over half of the attendees raise their hand. I always follow up with this question, "How many of you take advantage of your serger, using more than one stitch?" Far too many hands sheepishly come down. There are generally one or two brave souls that admit that they've never taken their purchase out of the box.

It is easy to become excited with the capabilities of a serger. The basic stitches save an inordinate amount of time, and the finished look is totally professional. On the creative side, knowing how to use your serger to add decorative embellishments makes this accessory machine even more attractive to own. Admittedly, sergers can be intimidating, and we could all use a serging buddy to help us get started.

Gail Yellen can be that buddy. Although she has years of teaching experience, she, too, was once a first-time serger owner and knows exactly what you need to learn to gain confidence in your serging skills. Through the pages of this book, she'll take you step by step through a variety of stitches, presser feet accessories, and thread options. Also look for advice on threading, tension, differential feed, and needles.

My recommendation is to initially peruse this book to check out the serging options—both creative and functional. Then, choose one stitch, technique, or accessory to master. Make sure you have a stack of sticky notes handy to make notes to yourself along the way, recording such things as settings, threads and fabrics you used. Take one of the sticky notes and flag Gail's handy Quick Reference Guide. You'll refer to that guide on many occasions.

After using this book, I know for certain that if you are asked if you use your serger, you'd reply with a resounding, "Absolutely!" Now go enjoy your serger!

introduction

SERGERS AREN'T ROCKET SCIENCE. Once you understand your serger's components, how they affect the stitch and improve your "operator technique," you'll be off and running (or serging) and wondering why you didn't love your serger sooner. These amazing machines can trim seam allowances and overlock the edges simultaneously, giving your projects clean-finished, strong seams and a professional appearance. They also offer loads of decorative potential.

How many times have you taken a serger class and come home with lovely samples of techniques that you can't replicate? You might have been instructed on how to set up your machine for a specific technique but not why. For instance, you've moved the left overlock needle to the right, disengaged the stitch finger (what is that?) or changed tension settings. But why did you make these adjustments?

In *Serger Essentials,* I will explain the key parts of your serger, how differential feed works and why you need to know how to fine-tune it, and how to set tensions properly. I also offer tips for using decorative threads, selecting needle and thread, and choosing helpful accessories. Scattered throughout the book, you'll find my Handy Tips & Techniques which I've developed over years of teaching. We've all had serger experiences where we've made all of the necessary adjustments correctly, yet the finished product is unsatisfactory. Why? Sometimes it's how we've handled the fabric—it's not the machine's fault! How we handle the fabric as we stitch is equally as important as correct machine setup. My Handy Tips & Techniques will help you avoid common mistakes.

Remember that not all sergers are created equal. They all have different capabilities, and results will vary with stitch quality, decorative techniques and threads. Your serger may have cover stitch and chain stitch capability, which will give you even more stitch options. Familiarize yourself with your serger's strengths and you'll get the most out of your machine and the best results.

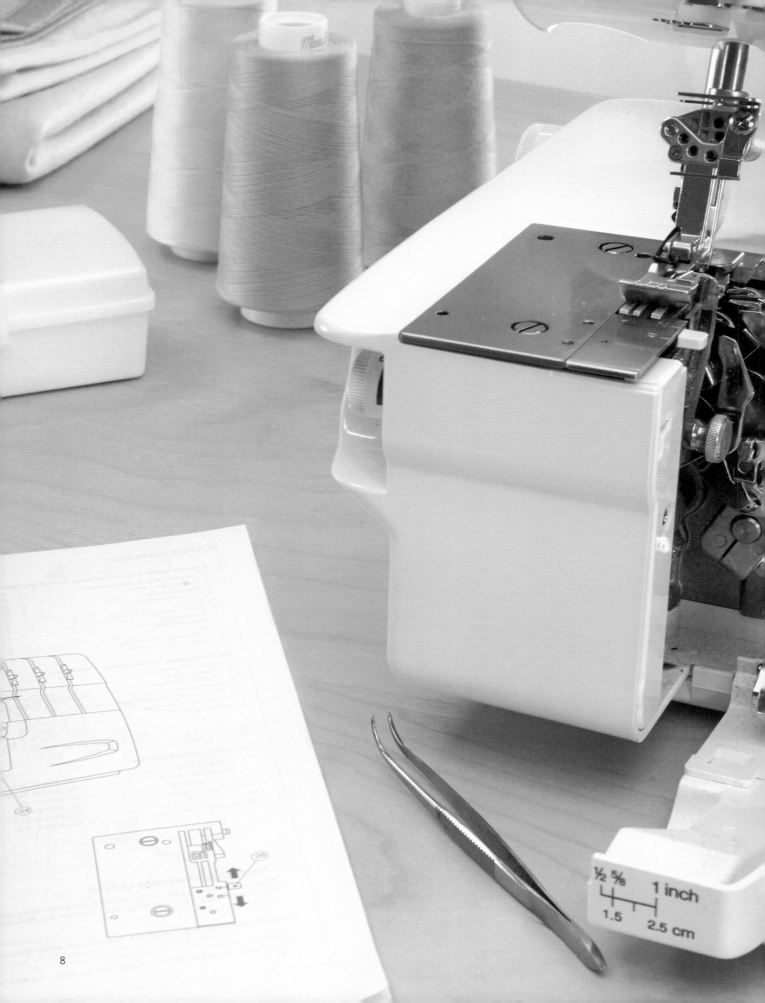

getting to know your serger

THIS SECTION covers everything you need to know about your serger, from setting it up to identifying and understanding the different components, and more!

Setting Up Your Serger

Understanding Serger Components

Useful Accessories

Serger Threads

Needles

Threading the Machine

Understanding the Stitch

The Differential Feed Factor

Setting Up Your Serger

FIRST THINGS FIRST: Take your serger out of the box. You'll also find an owner's manual in the box. Take it out and read it. It's loaded with information about your serger. The manufacturer will provide setting guides for the stitches, suggested needles and troubleshooting information, as well as other technical information to help you get the best performance from your machine. Think of these tensions, stitch lengths and cutting blade settings as suggested guidelines rather than hard and fast numbers. Sometimes you'll need to modify them.

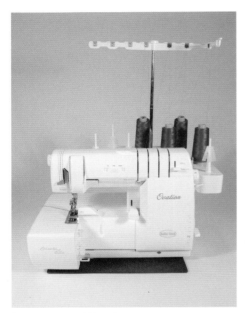

Serger on nonskid mat

Set up your serger in your sewing work space. Because sergers can stitch at a much faster rate than many home sewing machines, the machine may skitter around the work surface. Place your serger on a nonskid serger mat to reduce vibration, noise and movement. Plug in your power cord and foot control.

Handy Tips & Techniques

Buying a New Serger

If you're considering purchasing a new serger, do some comparison shopping. Buying a sewing machine or serger is similar to buying a car. A top-of-the-line serger will have more features, a variety of feet and accessories as well as a higher price. Explore different price points and decide whether spending a bit more might be worth it. If you aren't a serger expert yet but you plan to be, purchasing a machine that you can grow into is a good idea. As you gain confidence and skill, you may want those extra features that will allow you to expand your serger repertoire.

Sergers are available with a variety of features as well as numerous price points. Older models may have 3-thread stitches only, but now the most widely sold sergers are manufactured with a minimum of 4-thread stitch capability, and some have up to eight thread positions.

Four-thread sergers will have two overlock needle positions: an upper looper and a lower looper. These models will produce 3- and 4-thread wide and narrow overlock stitches. And if your machine has an upper looper converter or subsidiary looper, it will also stitch with two threads.

A serger that is overlock capable and cover/chain stitch capable will have a third looper—a chain looper. It will also have up to three cover/chain stitch needle positions. Several conversion steps are required to change from overlocking to cover stitching.

There are also "dedicated" cover/chain stitch machines. These machines have a chain looper only and won't overlock. Because fabric is never cut with this function, there is no knife. A cover/chain stitch machine is a great addition to the sewing room if you love your 4-thread serger but want to expand your serger possibilities.

Choosing the right serger is a personal decision; try out as many as you can before you decide which machine is right for you.

Understanding the Serger Components

NOW THAT YOUR SERGER IS SET UP, it's time to identify the different components that make up your machine and to learn what they do. The placement of some of the components may vary slightly from machine to machine; consult your manual if you have trouble locating or identifying the parts of your machine.

Cone Holders

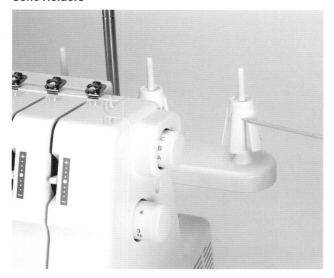

The platform on the back of your serger has cone holders for your thread. The cone holders are positioned closely behind the corresponding threading route.

What they do: As the name suggests, cone holders hold the serger thread steady and secure while you serge. If a cone of thread is placed over the spool pin only, the machine's vibration will cause it to bobble around, and the thread won't feed smoothly. Cone holders are removable and should be removed when you're using spools of all-purpose thread. Place a spool cap on top of all-purpose thread to help it feed properly.

Telescoping Antenna with Thread Guides

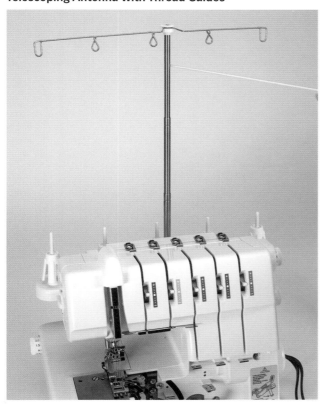

Fully extend the telescoping antenna. If it isn't fully extended, it can affect the thread tension. Your serger may have four to ten thread guides. (Older models may have three.)

What it does: The telescoping antenna is the first point on the threading route from the cone or spool. It ensures that the thread feeds up and off cones and spools properly. Each thread should be in the correct thread guide for its intended looper or needle.

Tension Control Dials or Levers

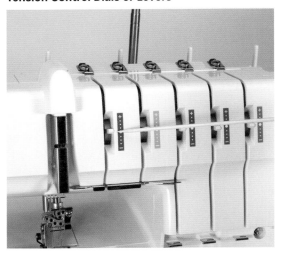

Recessed in each thread channel are the tension disks. The disks are controlled with corresponding tension control dials or levers.

What it does: The higher the tension level (indicated with a number on the dial or lever), the tighter the tension will be. Tensions are set according to the desired stitch and type of thread used. Your owner's manual will have suggested settings for various stitches, and many sergers designate normal tension settings with colors and/or brackets on the dials. If your machine is computerized, it may have buttons with + and – signs to raise or lower the settings. The tension disks should be open while threading so the thread will sit correctly between them. If the thread is not seated snugly between the disks, stitch formation will be loose.

Some sergers have a thread delivery system, not tension controls. The machine senses the amount of thread needed for correct formation of an overlock stitch.

Looper Air Threading

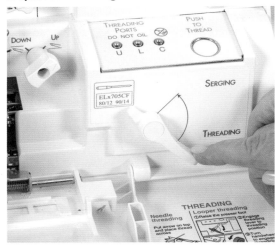

Several serger brands offer looper air-threading systems. This feature makes looper threading a breeze (pun intended). If you have any manual dexterity limitations, this feature might be worth having.

What it does: You insert the thread into a threading port and when it's activated, a burst of air whooshes the thread through tubes and through the looper eyes.

Speed Control Adjuster

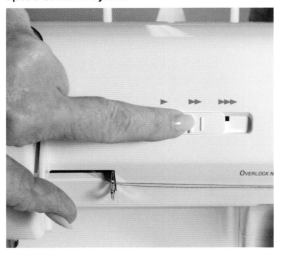

What it does: Some sergers have a speed control adjuster. This function allows you to control the maximum stitching speed. (It's a great feature for beginners.)

Presser Foot

What it does: Just as it does on your sewing machine, the presser foot holds the fabric in contact with the feed dogs, allowing the fabric to feed through as you stitch. Because a serger presser foot is significantly longer that a sewing machine's, it can sometimes be difficult to determine where the needle(s) will land on your fabric. Many standard feet have raised indicator ridges along the front edge or toe of the foot. These indicator ridges are aligned with the needle positions to help you position your fabric for accurate seam allowances. You'll learn more about the indicator ridges in Handy Tips & Techniques: Accurate Seam Allowances section.

Presser Foot Lifter

The location of the presser foot lifter will vary from machine to machine. Check your manual for the location on your machine.

What it does: The presser foot lifter raises and lowers the presser foot. You may also have an extra high lift to ease the positioning of thick, lofty fabrics under the foot. For many sergers, raising the presser foot also opens the tension disks.

Presser Foot Pressure Adjuster

If your machine has a presser foot adjuster, it will be on the top left or left side.

What it does: The factory preset pressure is usually perfect for most fabrics but may need to be decreased for very thick fabrics or increased for thin, lightweight ones to feed smoothly under the presser foot. Decreasing the pressure for stitching steep curves may also be helpful.

Feed Dogs

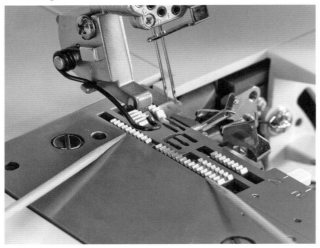

Under the presser foot are two sets of feed dogs—front and back. I've removed the presser foot here so you can see the feed dogs clearly.

What they do: The feed dogs move the fabric along under the foot as you stitch. The differential feed knob or lever adjusts the speed of the front feed dogs in relation to the back (whose speed remains constant).

Differential Feed Lever or Dial

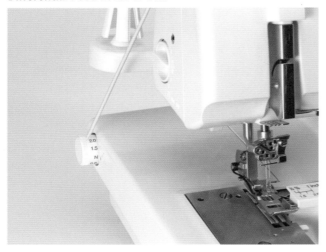

The location of the differential feed lever or dial will vary from machine to machine. Here, it's located on the back left side.

What it does: You can vary the speed of the front feed dogs with the differential feed control. This dial or lever will have numbers that range from 0.5–2.0; we'll explore this feature in depth later.

Cutting Blade or Knife

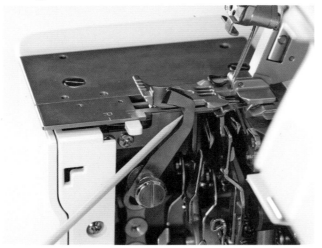

To the right of the presser foot is the cutting blade or knife. You'll likely need to open the front panel of your machine to see the knife.

What it does: There are two cutting blades or knives that work with each other to trim the fabric. One is stationary, and the other moves. As you move the knife to the left, you will trim off more of the fabric edge. Adjusting the knife to the right will trim off less. Knowing how to fine-tune the knife position is important. More about that later.

Loopers

Chain looper

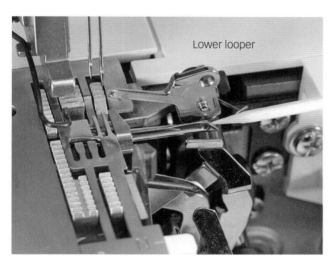

Lower looper

Upper looper

Open the front and side covers and look inside. Where is the bobbin? Sergers don't have bobbins. They have loopers.

What they do: Just as your sewing machine forms a stitch with the needle and bobbin threads, a serger forms a stitch with the needle(s) and looper threads. Think of the needle(s) and loopers as knitting needles. The stitch is formed between them as they interact with each other. (More about the stitch later.) Turn your handwheel toward you and you'll see the loopers move. They are positioned in alphabetical order from front to back. Here's an easy way to remember: get a CLU about your loopers (Chain, Lower, Upper). You might have two loopers if you don't have a chain stitch or cover hem feature.

Stitch Finger

The stitch finger is level with the serger bed just to the right of the needle(s). To disengage it, check your owner's manual.

What it does: The stitch finger is what the threads wrap around (between the needle[s] and loopers) to form a stitch. If you own an older model, you might have two stitch plates—standard and rolled hem. When engaged, the stitch finger is flush with the throat plate just to the right of the needles. The stitch finger is wider than the stitch pin and forms a wider stitch. It's similar to the large stitches formed on fat knitting needles and the small gauge stitches on thin needles.

Stitch Finger Control

What it does: This is just one of several types of stitch finger control. It will engage or disengage the stitch finger depending on whether you've selected a wide or narrow overlock stitch. Your manual will tell you how to operate this function on your machine.

Needles

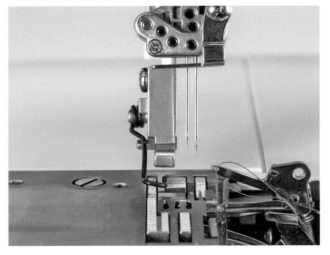

When serging, you'll need anywhere from one to three needles. The type of needle you use will depend on the fabric you're stitching. We'll review the different types of needles in a later section.

What it does: The needle and looper threads form the stitch. Depending on whether your machine has both overlock and cover/chain stitch functions, you may have up to five needle positions. There are two overlock and two or three cover/chain stitch positions.

Thread Guide

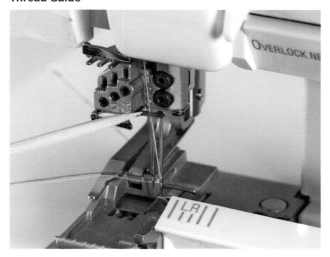

What it does: This is the final thread guide before threading the overlock needles. You'll notice another one in front of it for the cover/chain stitch needles. Having your thread in the right guide is key to a perfect stitch.

Stitch Width Dial

What it does: The stitch width dial allows you to control and fine-tune the width (from right to left) of an overlock stitch. On some sergers, it will move the stitch finger and knife simultaneously for perfect seam allowances under the stitches. Other models may have a separate knife position adjustor.

Stitch Length Control

The stitch length control on this machine is on the right side.

What it does: The stitch length control changes stitch lengths from short to long, just as it does on your sewing machine. Fabric and thread weights, seam strength and personal preference will determine the correct setting for your project.

Trim Bin

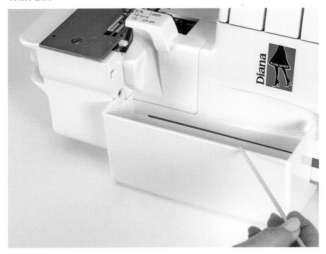

What it does: The trim bin catches threads and fabric as the knife trims them off. Empty it often to keep your machine and work area tidy.

Overlock Cover

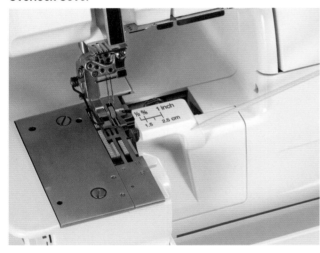

What it does: The overlock cover is designed to allow the knife and upper looper to function while overlocking. It also helps prevent fabric from getting tangled in the loopers. Yours may have seam allowance guides for positioning the fabric edge.

Hand Wheel

What it does: The handwheel raises and lowers the needles and moves the loopers. Turn it toward you when changing their positions.

Power Cord

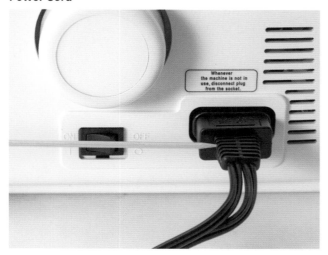

What it does: If your machine doesn't turn on, be sure the power cord is snugly attached to your serger (and electric outlet).

Power Switch

What it does: This one's pretty self-explanatory: Flip the switch to turn your machine on or off.

Foot Control

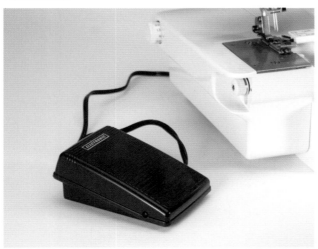

What it does: The foot control is like the accelerator in your car. Step on the pedal to begin stitching. The harder you press, the faster you'll stitch.

Useful Accessories

ACCESSORY FEET AND ATTACHMENTS

Watch any of the home improvement and woodworking TV shows and you'll notice that the craftsman always has just the right tool for any technique. And the finished project is perfect! Having the right tool for any job makes the results faster, easier and more accurate, and serger feet are no exception. When topstitching or stitching in the ditch on my sewing machine, having a foot with a guide blade to glide along the fabric's edge or seam makes all the difference between pretty good (with the standard foot) and perfect results. The variety of serger specialty feet and accessories has grown and varies according to your serger's make and model. Check with your sewing machine dealer or on your brand's website to see which ones are available for your serger.

Specialty feet (from left to right): Beading, blind hem, cording, chain/cover stitch, curve, elastic, lace applicator, pintuck, ruffler

Remember: Just because a foot has a specific name, doesn't mean it serves only one function. Many feet can multitask and are very useful for numerous techniques. Practice using different feet for different purposes. You'll develop a feel for positioning your fabric properly under the foot with practice and patience. Different fabrics may require slight adjustments, so test samples are suggested.

Your serger feet might not look exactly like the ones in the photograph, but they will have similar characteristics. The Specialty Serger Feet section at the end of the book gives you an in-depth look at the various accessory feet available and how to use them to give your projects a more professional look.

OTHER ACCESSORIES

Lots of helpful tools can make your serging successful. Here's a list of my favorites; some of these may come with your machine.

- Serger tweezers (1): These help access those hard-to-reach looper thread guides and lots of other uses.
- Lint brush (2): If you're new to serging, you'll be amazed at how much lint can accumulate when serging fleece and other fabrics. Keep your serger clean by brushing it out or vacuuming frequently.
- Vacuum mini tips (3): These attachments suction tight areas. Vacuum as you blow in compressed air. The vacuum grabs the loose lint and prevents it from being blown deeper into the serger.

- Compressed (canned) air (4): The long straw that attaches to the nozzle blow dusts and lint from hard-to-reach areas.
- Seam Sealant (5): Fray Check and Fray Block are both great sealants. Fray Check dries with a harder bead and is my preference for rolled hem napkin corners because they are laundered so frequently.
- Bodkin or double-eyed needle (6): This tool makes securing a thread tail under the stitches or between fabric layers a snap.
- Needle holder (7): Use this to hold needles while inserting them in the needle bar.
- Foam pads (not pictured): Place these on the spool pins to hold thread spools or cones securely, and to prevent thread from pooling under cones or spools.

- Spool caps (8): These allow thread to unwind from spools properly and help avoid snagging on spool edges.
- Looper threader (not pictured): An excellent tool for threading certain specialty threads through a looper eye.
- Thread nets (9): These aid smooth feeding of decorative threads and help prevent thread from getting caught under spools.
- Handy accessory case (10): Store your small accessories in a case to find them quickly.
- Notebook and page protectors (11): Building up a reference library of samples with settings recorded will prove invaluable. Keep samples of fabrics and threads that didn't work well for a particular technique—you'll learn a lot from these too.

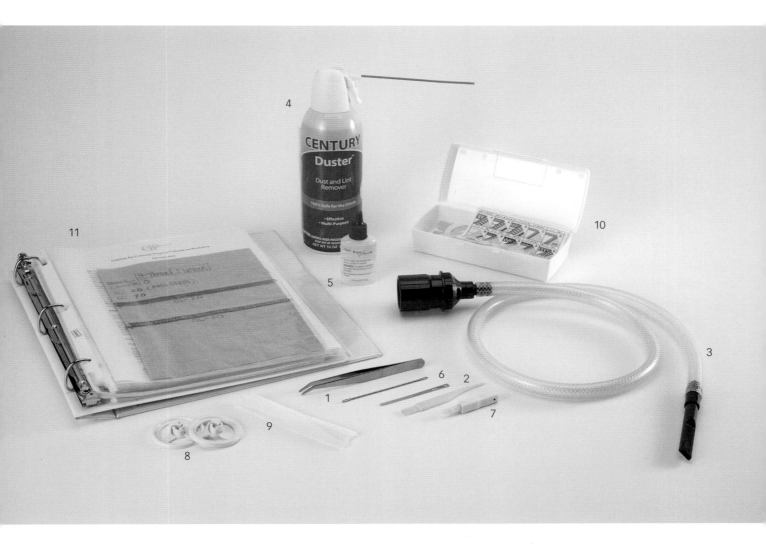

Serger Threads

THE MOST WIDELY USED SERGER CONE THREAD is two-ply polyester. It is one-third lighter than the spools of three-ply all-purpose thread used for sewing machines. The lighter weight reduces thread bulk in the seams, and high-quality threads withstand the higher stitching speed of sergers without as much breakage. Cotton-wrapped polyester thread will withstand higher pressing heat. Both are excellent choices for construction seams. You'll want to purchase four cones of the same color. If you're just starting out on a serger and are building your supplies, white, black, gray and beige are good basics. Gray blends well with many colors.

Use the best quality thread in your serger and sewing machine. "Bargain bin" threads have short staple fibers and may appear fuzzy with lint on the cone. These threads tend to break easily and build up problematic amounts of lint in your machine. Slubs or bumps in the thread can cause tension problems and poor stitch quality.

Can you use spools of all-purpose thread on a serger? Yes. Serger cone thread is available in a variety of colors but not as many as all-purpose thread. If an exact match to your fabric is desired, use the latter. If you do choose spools of all-purpose thread, purchase enough to complete your project.

Storing serger cones on a mounted thread rack is useful for quick access. Direct sunlight may fade some threads. Covering threads with a piece of cotton and keeping them out of the sun will prevent them from fading and collecting dust.

SPECIALTY AND DECORATIVE THREADS

The variety of decorative threads keeps growing, and sergers can stitch with many that a sewing machine can't. Many sergers perform beautifully with all types of specialty threads; however, some machines may not. You will need to test decorative threads on your machine to check stitch quality. Find the ones that work well and produce a good stitch on your serger.

Specialty threads are available in many fibers: cotton, polyester, rayon, acrylic, wool, metallic and nylon. You can even use fusible thread in the lower looper. As you familiarize yourself with these threads, you'll note that they have a range of textures, too: smooth, twisted, stretchy, soft, coarse. Some are too heavy to use in the needle but work very well in the upper, lower and chain loopers. Some decorative threads are very thick. Although you may be able to thread them through the loopers, if your serger is straining and you feel resistance, stop stitching. The thread may be too heavy and you don't want to damage your machine.

Handy Tips & Techniques

Ironing Decorative Threads

When ironing decorative threads, protect them with a press cloth. Woolly Nylon and other synthetic threads may melt or be damaged by an iron set on high heat.

Whether it's in the needle or loopers, thread should have uniform thickness. Novelty threads and yarns that vary thick and thin segments may cause tension problems and poor stitch quality. Lightweight threads like rayon or polyester embroidery threads are excellent for rolled hems. Heavier, bolder threads are great for flatlocking and decorative edging on projects.

Stitch at a moderate speed with specialty threads. Metallic threads may break more easily in the lower looper because there are more thread guides. You may want to try several different brands to compare strength and performance.

There are so many gorgeous threads (too many to list), but a few of my favorites include: Jeans Stitch, 12-weight cotton quilting threads, pearl crown rayon, solid and variegated threads, Woolly Nylon and Woolly Nylon Extra. Keep track of your stitch samples in a binder so that you can easily find your own favorites. It's also a good idea to keep track of thread that didn't stitch well on your serger.

These are just a few of the hundreds of decorative threads widely available. Threads shown here include pearl crown rayon, Woolly Nylon, Jeans Stitch, metallic, pearl cotton, variegated serger yarn and rayon braid.

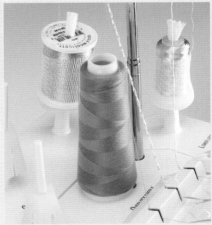

Handy Tips & Techniques

Use a Thread Net

Slippery decorative threads tend to relax and fall under the spool. If this happens, use a thread net. Rayon and some metallic threads often need nets to keep them feeding smoothly. Thread nets may affect the tension of your stitching, so test the tension settings on scrap fabric.

Needles

CONSULT YOUR OWNER'S MANUAL for suggested needles. Many serger brands recommend the EL x 705 needle. It was developed specifically for sergers, but it's not the only needle that will work well. Your sample fabric will show you whether you need to change the size and/or type of needle. Most sergers will work well with universal needles on woven fabrics. For many knit fabrics, especially those with Lycra, a stretch needle may prevent skipped stitches and form a better stitch. When using heavy decorative thread in the needles, insert a topstitch needle. The deeper groove along the shaft and larger eye are designed to hold thick threads.

Handy Tips & Techniques

Inserting Needles

If you just inserted fresh needles or changed needle positions and suddenly your serger isn't forming a stitch, don't panic. Check to be sure that the needles are correctly inserted in the needle bar. Even if they're a tiny bit too low, the serger won't form a stitch. If you are having difficulty fully inserting a single needle, you may need to loosen the screw for the needle position next to it. Some needle bars have narrow channels and need more room to correctly position the needle.

Be sure to tighten the screws that hold the needles in the needle bar when you remove or change a needle position. The vibrations produced when you stitch can rattle a screw out of its home, and because screws are so tiny, you may never find it!

You've probably noticed that the left needle is slightly higher than the right one. That's correct placement. If your needles are level with each other, one or both are not fully inserted. Loosen the screws and re-insert them.

Use tweezers or a needle holder while inserting needles and tightening the screws.

CORRECT: Left needle is slightly higher than the right.

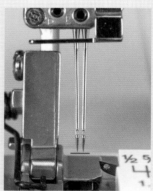

INCORRECT: Needles are level with each other.

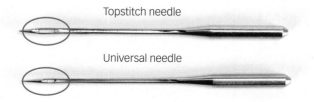

Topstitch needle

Universal needle

Insert fresh needles for every four hours of stitching. Polar fleece and dense fabrics (sweatshirt fleece, corduroy, velour) will dull needles more quickly. Most sergers are timed for a size-14 needle, but you can use a smaller size for lightweight fabrics. Never insert larger than size-16 needles.

Handy Tips & Techniques

Make a Sample

Always make a sample (or several) prior to stitching your project. Doing so can prevent ruining the project. Your sample should match the project. If you'll be serging a seam through two layers of fabric fused with interfacing, prepare the sample fabric in the same manner. Even a tissue-thin fusible interfacing can alter the correct differential feed or stitch length settings.

WHAT YOUR SAMPLE TELLS YOU

Needles: Are they the correct type and size for your fabric? Does the stitch formation look correct? You may need fresh or different needles. Switching from universal to stretch needles for some knit fabrics can make a big difference.

Tension settings, differential feed and stitch length: If you need to make any changes, there's no need to rip out stitches. You're working on scrap fabric! Make the necessary adjustments and stitch another sample. Samples are a real time (and project) saver. When stitching knits, test the differential feed on both the lengthwise and crosswise direction. You may need to raise the setting on the crosswise direction that has more stretch.

Create a sample binder: Save your samples with notes on settings, fabric type, etc., store in plastic page protectors and put them in a three-ring binder. You'll quickly build an excellent reference book specific to your machine. It's also helpful to keep samples of techniques or threads that did not work well. We think we'll remember these details months later…but not always. A sample will help.

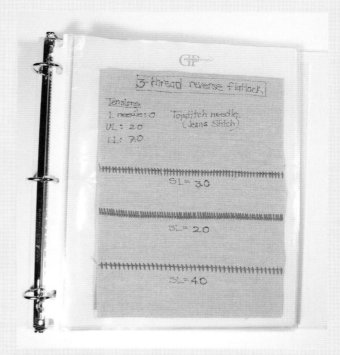

Binder page showing stitch samples for 3-thread reverse flatlock stitch.

Threading the Machine

NOW THAT YOU HAVE AN UNDERSTANDING of the different components that make up your serger, it's time to thread your machine. The exact method of threading may vary from machine to machine, but the general concept is the same. See your owner's manual for specific threading directions for your machine.

Thread your machine with the presser foot up (Figure 1). This opens the tension disks. Place your threads through the thread guides on the fully extended antenna (Figure 2). Using a flossing motion, slide the threads securely between the tension disks (Figures 3 and 4).

When threading the loopers and needles, most sergers have a specific sequence to follow. This sequence helps keep the threads parallel to each other. If the threads crisscross each other, at least one will break when you begin stitching. Before threading, check the positions of the upper and lower loopers. They should be separated, not in front of each other.

Your serger may have color-coded threading routes for the needles and loopers. This makes finding the corresponding thread guides easier. Consult your manual or threading diagram for

Figure 1

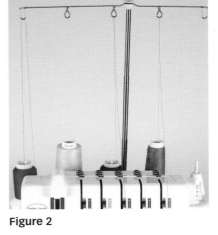
Figure 2

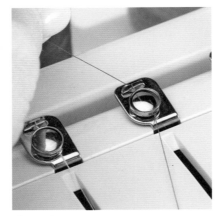
Figure 3

Figure 4

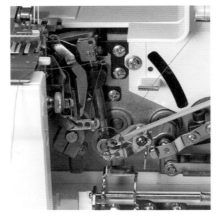
Figure 5

Figure 6

Handy Tips & Techniques

Use Tweezers!

When your fingers are just a bit too big, serger tweezers are very helpful for sliding thread into those hard-to-reach looper thread guides (especially the lower looper).

correct threading. Thread the loopers first (the green and blue thread in the photos) following the threading routes (Figures 5 and 6).

After the loopers, thread the right needle, then the left (yellow and red thread in the photo) (Figure 7). If you're a new serger owner, take your time. Thread and rethread several times to get comfortable with the process. It takes some practice, but after a few times, you'll be much more confident.

The "final exam" for correct threading is when you put the presser foot down and chain off (Figure 8). If your serger won't form stitches or a thread breaks, it's probably due to a threading error. Clip all of the threads and begin again from the thread cones. Check your machine's threading diagram to be sure you haven't skipped a guide. (Some sergers have a diagram inside the front cover.)

AIR THREADING

Some sergers have an air-threading feature. A jet of air is activated with either a push button or lever that pushes the threads through tubes and right into the eyes of the loopers. It's fast, easy and eliminates the need for threading in a specific order. It's especially helpful if you have any manual dexterity limitations. Follow the instructions for your model (Figure 9).

Figure 7

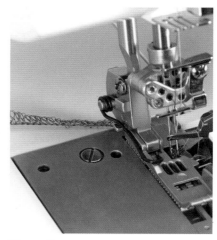

Figure 8

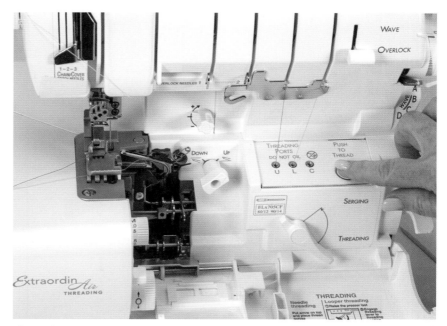

Figure 9

TYING ON LOOPER THREADING

If your machine is already threaded, you can rethread without starting from scratch. Although it's the easiest way to change looper threads, don't rely solely on this method. Why? If your looper thread breaks close to the needle, there won't be a thread tail to tie onto.

To use this method, raise the presser foot. Clip the looper thread close to the antenna thread guide (Figure 10). Remove that thread cone and replace it with the new one. Tie your new thread to the previous one and knot it once (Figure 11). Gently pull the threads one at a time through the machine (Figures 12 and 13). If the knot won't slide through the looper eye, clip it off and thread it through manually. This method is not recommended for air threading. The knot might not slide through the tubes (especially with thicker decorative threads).

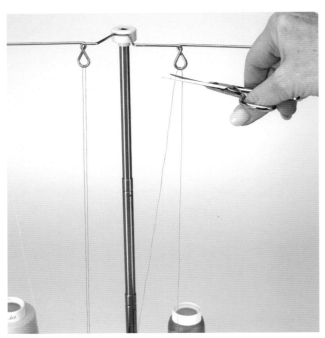

Figure 10

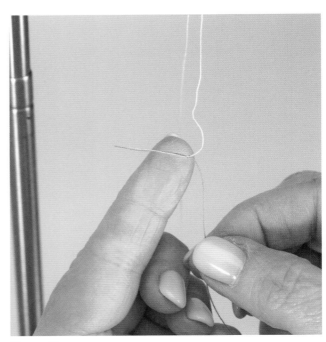

Figure 11

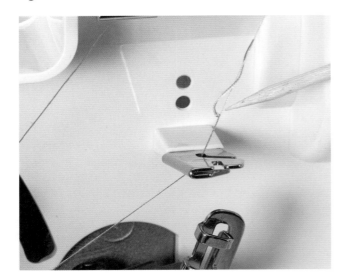

Figure 12

Figure 13

THREADING DECORATIVE THREADS

Depending on their thickness and texture, decorative threads can present challenges when threading. An example of this is Woolly Nylon. It's very durable, soft and fuzzy in a relaxed state but almost impossible to thread through a looper (without some help). It's time to use a looper threader. Your machine may have included a wire with a loop on one end, but if not, a dental floss threader or a "leader thread" (a long piece of all-purpose thread) will work nicely. Place the cut ends of the threader or "leader thread" through the looper eye. Insert several inches of the decorative thread through the threader loop (no knot required), and pull through the looper eye (Figures 14 and 15).

For air-threading tubes, cut one yard (0.9m) of serger cone thread and fold it in half. Insert the cut ends into the threading port and hold onto the looped end. Push the threading button or lever. The cut ends will appear in the looper eye (Figure 16). Insert several inches of the decorative thread through the threader loop (no knot required) and pull gently through the looper eye (Figures 17 and 18).

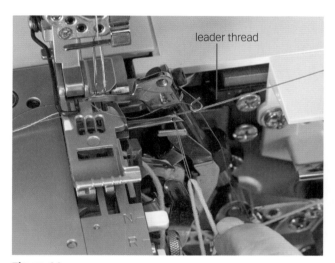

Figure 14

Figure 15

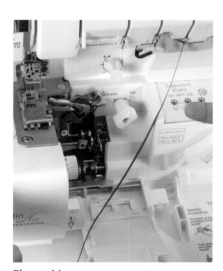

Figure 16

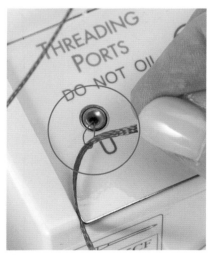

Figure 17

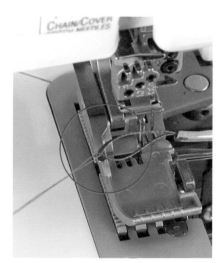

Figure 18

NOW THAT YOU'VE PRACTICED, you should be somewhat comfortable setting up your machine, threading it and chaining off. You have a basic understanding of the different parts that make up your machine and the necessary accessories to get you serging. In order to fully understand your serger, let's take a closer look at the basic 4-thread overlock stitch and how the various components work together to make a balanced stitch.

4-THREAD OVERLOCK STITCH

The 4-thread overlock is a balanced stitch. The fabric lies smooth and flat under the threads, and the loops meet precisely on the fabric edge. If your machine has color-coded threading routes, thread the loopers and needles with the corresponding color. This is a quick way to identify which thread is which. In this example:

Left Needle = red; Right Needle = yellow

Upper Looper = green; Lower Looper = blue

On the upper side of the fabric, the left and right needle threads will form two parallel rows of straight stitches. The left needle stitches create the seam. On the underside of the fabric, the right needle stitches appear as shorter dots. The upper looper thread forms the loops on the top or upper side of the fabric. The lower looper forms the loops on the under or lower side of the fabric. (When stitching a 3-thread overlock with a single needle [right or left position], that thread will form the seam.)

Left needle thread (red)

Right needle thread (yellow)

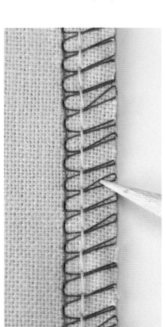

Upper looper thread (green)

Lower looper thread (blue)

UNDERSTANDING TENSION

One of the key factors in getting a perfectly formed stitch is tension. First, the needle and looper threads must be correctly engaged in their tension disks. Because a serger's tension disks are recessed, even an experienced sewist can occasionally miss engaging the thread in the disks. To make sure the threads are properly positioned in the disks, raise the presser foot. This will open the tension disks. Hold the thread taut between your hands and use a flossing motion to slide the thread between the disks (Figure 1). Follow the threading route and insert the threads in the needle and looper eyes.

Many serger brands will designate normal tension settings by highlighting them with different colors or bracketing on the dial or lever. If your serger is computerized and auto-sets the tension, when you turn it on, it will default to normal tension settings.

ADJUSTING TENSION

For a balanced stitch, start with all tension settings on normal. Stitch a sample. If the stitch formation isn't correct, try to determine which thread needs an adjustment. Raise or lower the setting one number at a time. For example, if the left needle tension is set on 2 and it's too loose, raise it to 3. The higher the number, the tighter the tension. The lower the number, the looser the tension.

Don't change more than one tension setting at a time. It makes it hard to determine which adjustment solved the original problem. (You may have to adjust more than one tension setting, but do them individually.)

Some serger models don't have traditional tension systems. They have thread delivery systems that sense the weight and thickness of the fabric and thread. A stitch selector lever makes adjustments according to which needles and stitch are being used. When you open the front cover, you may see a fine-tuning knob to adjust looper tensions for specialty threads and/or fabrics.

Figure 1

The normal tension setting is designated with a dot on each of the tension dials.

Upper Looper Tension Too Loose

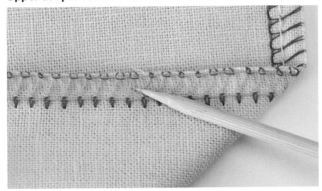

If the upper looper tension is too loose, the loops (green thread) will be pulled to the underside of the fabric. Increase the upper looper tension in small increments until the loops meet the edge of the fabric.

Upper Looper Tension Too Tight

If the upper looper tension is too tight, the lower looper thread (blue thread) will be pulled to the right side of the fabric. Decrease the upper looper tension until the loops meet at the edge of the fabric.

Lower Looper Tension Too Loose

If the lower looper tension is too loose, the loops will be pulled to the right side of the fabric. Increase the lower looper tension in small increments until the loops meet at the edge of the fabric.

Lower Looper Tension Too Tight

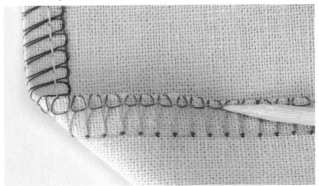

If the lower looper tension is too tight, the upper looper thread will be pulled to the underside of the fabric. Decrease the lower looper tension until the loops meet at the edge of the fabric.

Needle Tension Too Loose

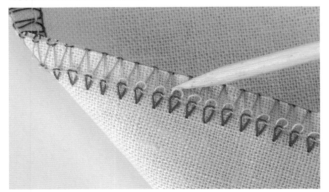

If the needle threads form loops on the underside of the fabric and "ladders" appear in the seam, tighten the needle tension.

Needle Tension Too Tight

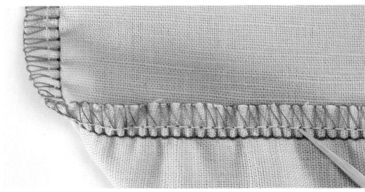

When the needle tension is too tight, the fabric will pucker on the left side of the stitch. Loosen the needle tension that forms the seam.

NOT A TENSION PROBLEM

Did you know that the knife position on most sergers is adjustable? If you've adjusted all of the tension settings, the loops meet on the fabric edge, but if your fabric is still scrunching up under the stitches or the loops are hanging off the edge of the fabric, it might not be a tension problem. You may need to reposition your knife. If the fabric is wrinkled and crowded under the stitching, the knife isn't trimming off enough fabric (Figure 2). Turn the dial or knob to move the knife to the left to trim off more fabric. Continue to make this adjustment until the loops meet at the fabric edge and the fabric lies flat under the stitches.

If the loops are hanging off the fabric edge, the knife is trimming off too much fabric (Figure 3). Move the knife to the right to trim off less fabric. Check your owner's manual for how to adjust the knife position.

SPECIALTY THREADS AND TENSION

The variety of specialty threads that look beautiful and work well in sergers is wide. These threads vary in thickness, surface texture and fiber content, and some can be used for construction as well as decorative purposes. Ajdusting the tension for each thread is necessary for a perfect stitch. Very thick, coarse threads may require a lower tension setting. And lighter, smoother threads may require a higher setting. Test samples will help you fine-tune the settings.

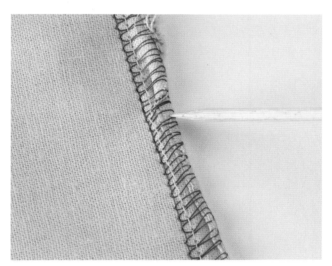

Figure 2

Figure 3

Handy Tips & Techniques

Stitching Heavy or Stiff Fabrics

Sometimes when stitching stiff or heavy fabric (like denim or upholstery fabrics), "ladders" appear in the seam from the right side (Figure 4). Tighten the tension on the needle position that forms the seam. If your machine doesn't have tension adjustment dials, reinforce the seam on your sewing machine.

Figure 4

STITCH WIDTH

Several factors determine your stitch width:

- The first is **needle position**. When your needle is in the left position for a 4-thread or 3-thread overlock stitch, your serger will form the widest stitch. The stitch width is the same with or without the right needle. When you remove the left needle and use the right needle only, the stitch width is approximately 2 millimeters narrower. You've automatically narrowed the stitch width. The looper threads don't have to grab onto that left thread.

- The second factor determining stitch width is the **stitch finger**. The stitch finger is between the needle(s) and loopers. (On some sergers, the stitch finger can be adjusted right or left to fine-tune the stitch width.) When engaged, the stitch is formed over it. It's like wrapping thread around all four fingers on your hand (Figure 5). Stitching a narrow 3-thread overlock with the stitch finger engaged is like wrapping thread around three fingers. Without the stitch finger, it's like wrapping thread around two fingers. If the stitch finger is disengaged, the stitch forms over a thin stitch pin, forming a narrower stitch. Stitching with the left needle and the stitch finger engaged produces the widest stitch. When the right needle only is in place and the stitch finger is disengaged, the narrowest stitch is formed.

- There is one more adjustment that will narrow the stitch a bit more: changing the **tension settings** for a rolled hem. We'll explore the rolled hem in a later section.

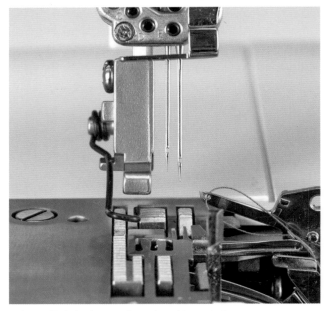

Left needle is in place to form the widest stitch

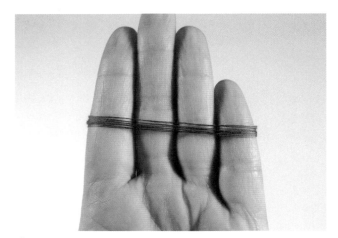

Figure 5

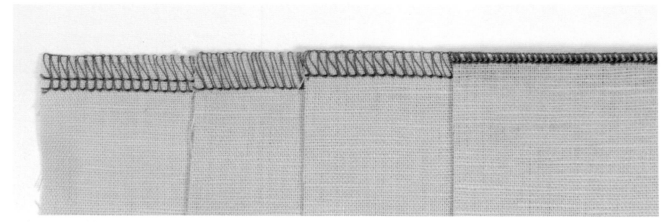

Various stitch widths, from left to right: 4-thread overlock; 3-thread wide overlock; 3-thread narrow overlock; 3-thread rolled hem

STITCH LENGTH

You're probably familiar with adjusting stitch length on a sewing machine. You do it all the time. Fabric weight and type (knit or woven), seam strength and personal preference dictate stitch length settings. For fabric that is loosely woven, frays easily or is lightweight, a shorter stitch length provides more fabric coverage on raw edges. A longer stitch length works well on sweatshirt fleece, polar fleece, velour and other thick, lofty fabrics. If the stitch length is too short, it may be difficult for the feed dogs to advance heavy fabric under the presser foot. Knit fabrics don't fray, so edge coverage isn't critical.

Stitch Length and Thread Weight

Here's a visual to illustrate the concept of how thread weight affects stitch length. If three very large adults are sitting next to each other in the economy seats on an airplane, chances are there isn't a speck of room between them. They are probably crowding into each other's space. Three small children in the same seats will be comfortable with plenty of space between them. That's the difference between thick, heavy threads and lightweight serger cone or all-purpose threads. Thick threads need more space for stitches to sit comfortably next to each other and prevent stacking. Stacking is when stitches bunch up and overlap each other because the stitch length is too short. The stitch appearance can vary considerably with the exact same settings from one thread or fabric type to another.

Another factor to consider is seam strength. If your stitches are too far apart, the seam may be weak. To test your seam strength, cut two pieces of scrap fabric and stitch them together. Gently pull on the pieces to check the seam strength. If the seam is weak or loose, shorten the stitch length and test again.

When stitching with specialty threads, there isn't a right or wrong stitch length setting. You're the designer. For decorative edges, as long as the stitches aren't stacking, the fabric supports them and you like the appearance, then that's the right setting.

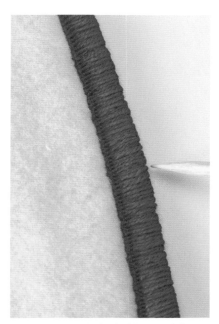

This edge was stitched with 11-weight polyester decorative thread. The 1.5mm stitch length provides dense, complete edge coverage without stitch stacking on lofty polar fleece.

These heavy linen edges were all stitched on the same stitch length—2.5—but with various weights and types of threads. Notice the difference in coverage when stitched with 40-weight embroidery thread and serger cone thread compared to heavier, thicker 11-weight decorative threads.

The Differential Feed Factor

DIFFERENTIAL FEED is one of the best features on a serger. Understanding what differential feed does and how to adjust it correctly for various fabrics, grain lines and techniques will give you accurate professional results. And you'll stop avoiding certain fabrics because of previous poor results (like stretchy knits)!

Raising the differential feed setting means that the front feed dogs can feed stretchy fabric (knits) or unstable bias grain lines on woven fabric under the foot faster than the back feed dogs advance it out. This is similar to manually pushing fabric under the foot of a sewing machine as you sew to prevent stretching. A differential feed setting of 2.0 means that the front feed dogs are working twice as fast as the back set. By turning the differential feed below 1.0 or N to 0.5, the front feed dogs are slowed down to half the speed of the back ones. This is similar to taut sewing—holding fabric taut from the front and back of the presser foot as you sew to prevent puckering.

In addition to compensating for stretchy fabrics, manipulating the differential feed also allows you to create decorative techniques such as a lettuce leaf edge and gathering. More on those techniques a bit later.

HOW TO DETERMINE YOUR DIFFERENTIAL FEED SETTING

The best way to get familiar with how to manipulate the differential feed is to actually do it! Dig through your stash and pull out leftover knit fabrics (possibly from past projects that were duds because you didn't know then what you know now about your serger). It's a terrific way to fine-tune your differential feed know-how, as well as learn how to handle fabric correctly while stitching.

Stitch lots of test samples. As you become familiar with different types of knit fabrics, you'll find yourself automatically knowing whether to start at a 1.0 or N setting, or to immediately jump to a higher one. The variety of knit fabrics and fibers has grown exponentially over the last few years. Each fabric has its own personality when sewn, so it's important to get to know its characteristics with samples prior to starting on your project.

The differential feed setting that is correct on the lengthwise (more stable) direction of knit fabrics will probably be different than that on the crosswise (stretchier) direction. Cut several sets of 10" × 3" (25.4cm × 7.6cm) strips both in the

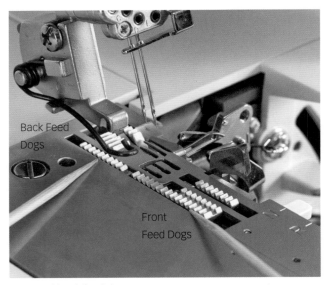
Front and back feed dogs

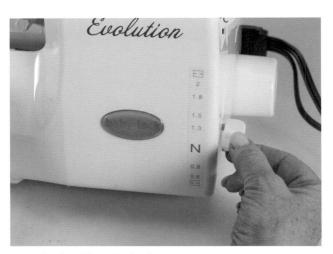
Start with the differential feed at N or 1.0

crosswise and lengthwise direction from your scrap project fabric. The sample should always match the project technique for accuracy. Remember that the number of layers can make a difference. If you're testing the differential feed for seam construction, put two strips together for testing. If you're finishing a single edge, use one fabric strip. Experiment with different settings.

Here's a wonderful learning opportunity to really see how much of a difference differential feed can make. On the lengthwise strips, begin with the differential feed setting on 1.0 or N. Stitch the edge and evaluate it. If the edge is wavy and longer than 10" (25.4cm), you'll need to speed up those front feed dogs by raising the setting. Try 1.5 next. Stitch and compare results. If the edge looks better but is still wavy and slightly longer, turn up the setting to 2.0. On your third sample, stitched with the setting at 2.0, if the edge is puckered and slightly shorter than 10" (25.4cm), that's the correct setting.

Bottom: Differential feed set at N: Edge is stretched

Middle: Differential feed set at 1.5: Edge is better, but still slightly stretched

Top: DIfferential feed set at 2.0: Edge is perfect

serger stitches, techniques and projects

IN THIS SECTION, we'll learn about the various stitches you can achieve with your serger and a few applications and techniques that use these stitches.

Start Serging

A FEW THINGS TO REMEMBER AS YOU GET STARTED: When sewing, always start with the fabric under the needle on your sewing machine. When overlocking, always "chain onto" the fabric. Begin by stitching a chain of several inches prior to the needles stitching in the fabric. For light- to medium-weight fabrics, lifting the toe of the foot and sliding the fabric under it without raising the presser foot is sufficient for the feed dogs to advance it (Figure 1). Thick fabrics need a little more help.

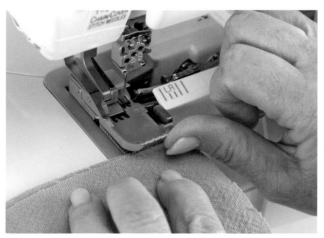

Figure 1

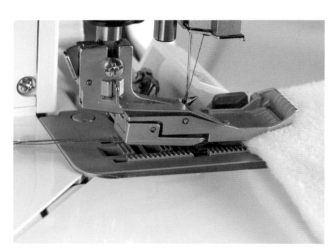

Figure 2

SERGING THICK FABRICS

When serging through thick, lofty fabrics such as batting, sweatshirt fleece or polar fleece, begin by serging a chain, then raise the presser foot to position the fabric under it. These fabrics and others of similar thickness occupy most, if not all, of the space under the raised foot. It might look as though the foot is down. Double-check that the presser foot is lowered before stitching (Figure 2). (Some machines won't stitch if it isn't.)

Handy Tips & Techniques

Thick Fabrics

Hang onto the thread chain behind the presser foot until the needle(s) have taken a few stitches in the fabric (Figure 3). This will help the fabric advance more easily.

Stitch at a moderate speed. The knife needs to cut through more bulk; allow the knife to trim the fabric cleanly by slowing down. It's the same concept as cutting through a stick of butter versus a piece of beef. A knife will cut through butter in a split second. When slicing a roast, it takes a bit more time to cut cleanly.

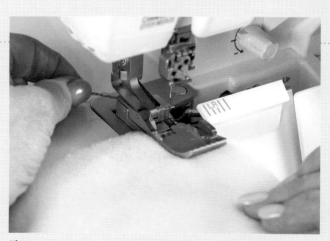

Figure 3

4-Thread Overlock Stitch

MACHINE SETUP

Presser foot: Standard
Left needle tension: Normal
Right needle tension: Normal
Upper looper tension: Normal
Lower looper tension: Normal
Stitch length: Variable 1.0–4.0
Differential feed: Variable depending on fabric type (Test lengthwise and crosswise when using knit fabric.)
Stitch finger: Engaged
Knife: Engaged

The 4-thread overlock stitch is a construction workhorse. While the left needle thread forms the seam, the right needle thread provides "construction insurance." This stitch's built-in strength and elasticity make it a good choice for sewing knit and woven fabric garments as well as other projects when seam strength is necessary. The left needle should be aligned at the designated seam allowance. Double-check your pattern for the correct seam allowance before stitching. If too much seam allowance is trimmed off, you can no longer let out the seam. Check your owner's manual for the correct width setting for the knife.

Handy Tips & Techniques

Accurate Seam Allowances

Here's an easy way to stitch an accurate seam allowance. Check the pattern's seam allowance and draw a line on scrap fabric the same distance from the raw edge. Place the line in front of the indicator ridge of the left needle for a 4-thread or 3-thread-wide stitch, or the right needle for a 3-thread narrow overlock seam. Note how much fabric the knife trims off. Mark the seam allowance at the edge of your project fabric and position it under the toe of the foot. Begin stitching. Watch the knife (not the needles) and trim off a consistent width from the fabric edge as you stitch. The seam allowance will be accurate.

When serging a garment, be sure it fits prior to stitching and trimming the seam allowances. If you've serged the seams and it's too snug, you may have to dream up a creative way to add fabric to the design!

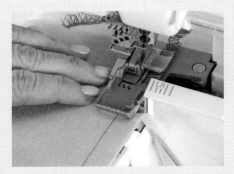

The left overlock needle forms the stitch so that ridge is aligned with the seam allowance line.

GATHERING: MACHINE SETUP

Presser foot: Standard
Left needle tension: 5–7.2 (Check the owner's manual)
Right needle tension: 5–7.2 (Check the owner's manual)
Upper looper tension: Normal
Lower looper tension: Normal
Stitch length: Longest possible 4.0
Differential feed: 2.0
Stitch finger: Engaged
Knife: Engaged

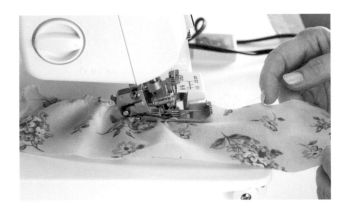

Not only can you manipulate the differential feed for construction purposes, you can create decorative effects with construction stitches. The 4-thread overlock is a terrific construction stitch, but with a couple of simple adjustments, it can gather fabric. The lighter the fabric, the more easily it will gather. Cut your sample fabric along the same grain line as your project. (The lengthwise, crosswise and bias grain lines may gather differently.)

Make a sample to determine how much fabric to allow for the desired finished ruffle. There isn't a standard formula. To calculate, cut a 20" (50.8cm) strip of scrap fabric. After gathering the edge, if it now measures 10" (25.4cm) (and has the desired amount of fullness), then cut twice the finished length plus at least 6" (15.2cm) more. Check your owner's manual for the suggested settings, but don't be afraid to adjust the needle tension settings higher or lower. Higher needle tensions will produce tighter gathers, while lower settings (but still above normal) will stitch looser gathers.

If your needle threads break, lower the settings slightly until breakage stops. Heavier fabric will not gather as easily, and you may have to tighten the gathering by pulling the needle threads. If your fabric is an upholstery velvet or similar weight, a traditional gathering method on the sewing machine may be a better choice.

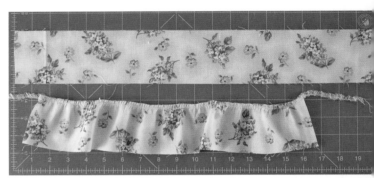

Tighten gathers

Loosen and Tighten Gathers

To loosen the gathers, gently pull the fabric outward along the thread chain on both ends and redistribute the gathers evenly.

To tighten the gathers, pull on the needle threads only. Use both ends of the thread chain and redistribute the gathers evenly.

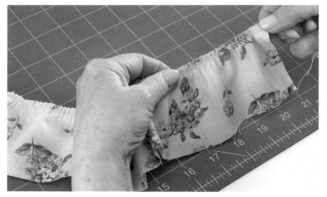

Loosen gathers

The Ruffler Foot

Did you know that you can gather a ruffle and attach it to flat fabric in one step on a serger? It's possible with a ruffling foot. The separator platform slot keeps the fabric you want to remain flat from contacting the feed dogs so the 2.0 differential feed setting doesn't gather it.

The fabric you do want to ruffle is positioned right-side up under the foot against the feed dogs. The flat fabric is positioned right-side down in the slot above the separator platform.

Most ruffling feet gather fabric at a 2:1 ratio, but that isn't exact. The weight and crispness of the fabric may alter the tightness of the gathers. Cut the ruffle fabric longer than double the desired finished length. Make a sample to determine how tightly the fabric gathers.

Figure 1

1 Prior to gathering, finish the bottom edge of the ruffle strip as desired. A rolled hem is a good option.

2 Raise the needles and presser foot. Slide the ruffle fabric under the needles. Lower the needles into the fabric to hold it in place (Figure 1).

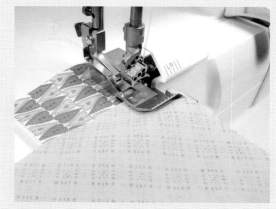

Figure 2

3 Slide the flat fabric into the foot slot up to the needles. Lower the foot (Figure 2).

4 Stitch at a moderate speed. For a uniform ruffle width, guide the fabric (without pulling) to keep it straight. The knife will trim off ⅛" (3mm) from the right edge (Figure 3).

5 Angle the top fabric slightly to the right while stitching. For tighter gathers, gently pull back on the flat fabric as you stitch.

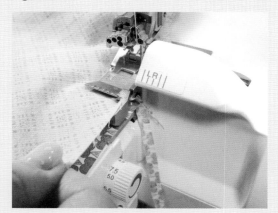

Figure 3

Easing a Sleeve Cap

Gathering is also a wonderful way to ease a sleeve cap evenly. You won't trim away any of the sleeve fabric, just "skim off the whiskers." Begin stitching close to the underarm sleeve seam with the differential feed set at 1.0 or N. When you reach the first notch, stop and reset the differential feed to 1.5 (Figure 4). Continue stitching at this setting around the cap to the next notch. Stop and reset the differential feed to 1.0 (Figure 5). Finish stitching the sleeve cap edge (Figure 6). (Depending on the amount to be eased, the gathering may need to be tightened or loosened. Leave enough thread chain on either end to adjust.)

You may notice that the loops hang off the fabric edge slightly. Don't bother making any adjustments because the stitches will be hidden in a seam.

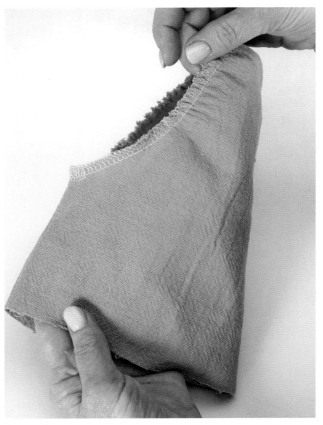

Figure 6

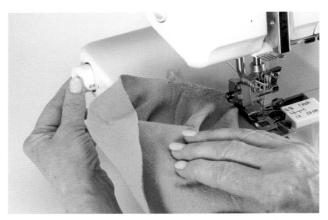

Figure 4

Figure 5

Handy Tips & Techniques

Skimming Off the Whiskers

"Skimming off the whiskers" refers to trimming away the threads on the raw edge of your fabric. You won't cut off any of the fabric.

The knife cuts away only the threads

Ease-Plus Gathering Method

If your fabric isn't gathering as tightly as you'd like using the traditional gathering method, or if you can't adjust your needle tension, try the ease-plus gathering method.

Place your left middle finger firmly against the back of the presser foot. Begin stitching. The fabric will bunch up against your finger (Figure 7). Continue exerting pressure against the presser foot until the fabric will not advance. Release that fabric. Repeat this process and finish gathering the fabric. (This method works well on your sewing machine, too.)

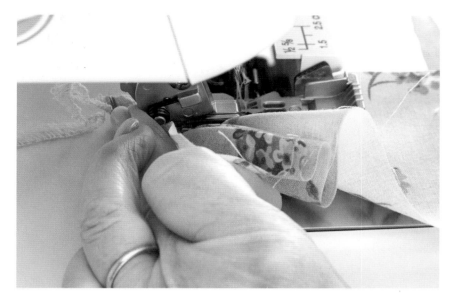

Figure 7

Handy Tips & Techniques

My Fabric Won't Gather!

While I was teaching the gathering technique at a hands-on serger workshop, a student raised her hand and said her fabric wasn't gathering at all, so there must be something wrong with her machine. The machine settings were correct. She stitched a new piece of the same fabric while I observed. After a couple of seconds, I asked her to stop and look at what her right index finger was doing. That one finger was exerting too much pressure and holding back the fabric. The front feed dogs couldn't advance the fabric fast enough to gather it. When she held the fabric lightly to guide it and let the differential feed setting do its job, the fabric gathered perfectly!

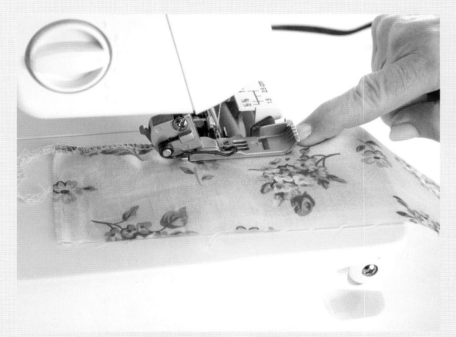

Right index finger pressure is preventing the fabric from advancing.

MACHINE SETUP

Presser foot: Standard
Left needle tension: Normal or Right needle tension: Normal
Upper looper tension: Normal
Lower looper tension: Normal
Stitch length: Variable 3.0–3.5
Differential feed: Variable depending on fabric type (test on knit fabric)
Stitch finger: Engaged
Knife: Engaged

Remove one needle and its thread, and you now have a 3-thread overlock stitch. With the needle in the left position, the width is the same as a 4-thread stitch; this is the 3-thread wide overlock. Change the needle and thread to the right position and your stitch is now a narrow 3-thread overlock. Both have more built-in stretch than the 4-thread overlock and are great for seams that don't require the added strength of the second row of stitches.

The 3-thread wide or narrow overlock is perfect for decorative edging on all types of projects. You can use decorative thread in your upper and lower loopers and coordinating color serger cone thread in the left or right needle for finishing exposed edges. It's a great way to dress up the edges on table runners or toppers, blankets, baby wraps and shawls. See the Decorative-Edge Basket Liner on page 56 for a simple project using the 3-thread narrow decorative overlock stitch.

Handy Tips & Techniques

Thread Guides

During a hands-on workshop, a student was having trouble forming a perfect 4-thread overlock stitch. After checking tension settings, etc., I looked at the thread positions in the guides above the needles. The threads were in the cover stitch needle guides—too far left of the overlock needle guides. The threads should be straight and directly above the needles. The same is true for 3-thread overlock stitches—make sure the thread is directly above the needles.

Threads in the correct thread guide for overlocking

Threads are in the cover stitch thread guide—incorrect thread guide for overlocking needles

3-THREAD NARROW HEM FOR FORMAL WEAR: MACHINE SETUP

Presser foot: Standard
Right needle tension: Normal
Upper looper tension: Normal
Lower looper tension: Normal
Stitch length: Variable 2.5
Differential feed: Variable (test on your fabric)
Stitch finger: Disengaged
Knife: Engaged

Have you ever had a spike high heel (or any heel with a sharp corner) snag a rolled hem and pull off a few inches? This is a great solution for long dresses, skirts, prom gowns and bridal wear. This technique creates a scant ¼" (6mm) hem that's secure and beautiful.

1 Thread the right needle and upper looper with matching color serger cone or all-purpose thread. Thread the lower looper with fusible thread (Figure 1). The right side of the fabric is face up when serging.

2 Skim off the whiskers as you stitch around the edge of the skirt (Figure 2). Clip off the thread chain.

3 Turn and press the stitched edge to the wrong side (Figure 3). The lower looper thread will fuse to the wrong side of the fabric.

4 On your sewing machine, set the straight stitch length to 3.0mm and stitch the hem in place (Figure 4).

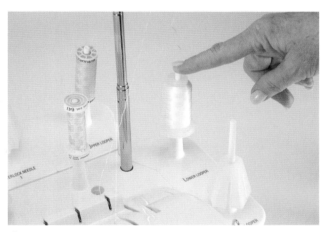

Figure 1

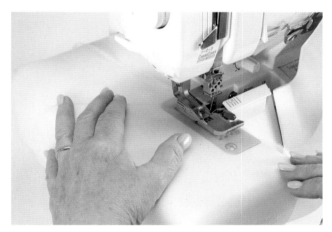

Figure 2

Figure 3

Figure 4

APPLYING RIBBING TO A T-SHIRT NECKLINE: MACHINE SETUP

Presser foot: Standard
Right needle tension: Normal
Upper looper tension: Normal
Lower looper tension: Normal
Stitch length: Variable 3.0
Differential feed: Approx. 1.5–variable depending on fabric (test on knit fabric)
Stitch finger: Engaged
Knife: Engaged

Flat-Construction Method

If you enjoy creating your own T-shirts and tops with ribbed necklines and bands around the bottom edges, either 3-thread stitch will work well, but a narrow 3-thread overlock is used on most ready-to-wear tops.

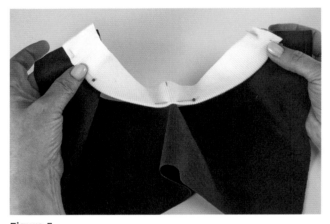

Figure 5

1 Serge the T-shirt's right shoulder seam and leave the left one open. Follow your pattern for the correct ribbing length. For finished ribbing 1"(2.5cm) wide, cut the width 2½" (6.4cm).

2 Fold the ribbing in half lengthwise, wrong sides together, and press. Fold the pressed ribbing in half and mark the center point on the raw edge. Fold each short edge to the center and mark the quarter points.

3 Fold the T-shirt front and back, and mark the center point on both sides. Mark the quarter points by matching the center marks. (Sometimes the shoulder seams are the quarter points, but measure to be sure.)

4 Matching the raw edges, pin the ribbing to the neckline at the marks. Pin close to and parallel to the folded edge (Figure 5). (This method prevents stitching over the pins.)

5 Raise the presser foot to get all three layers under the foot smoothly. Stitch with the ribbing face up.

6 After the needle has taken 2 stitches through the fabrics, stop. Pinch the fabrics at the first mark and stretch the ribbing to match the neckline edge length. Don't stretch the neckline of the T-shirt. Stitch to the first pin, then stop (Figure 6).

7 Repeat these steps to complete the neckline ribbing. Stitch the shoulder seam and ribbing closed on the left side.

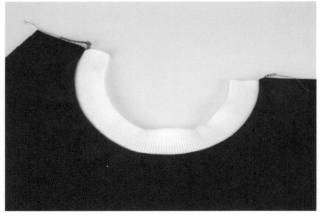

Figure 6

Finished collar

Quartering Method

Though flat construction might be easier, it tends to create a bulky seam at the junction of the ribbing and neckline. The quartering method takes a few more minutes to do, but the finished product is very professional. (Use this method for the band bottom, too.) You'll use the same machine setup used for the flat-construction method.

1 Serge both shoulder seams with a 3-thread overlock stitch over stay tape or ribbon to stabilize the shoulder seams.

2 Stitch the short edges of the ribbing together, right sides together, on your sewing machine. Press the seam allowance open (Figure 7). Fold the ribbing in half lengthwise with wrong sides together, and press.

3 Fold in half on the seam, and mark the center front. Match center front and back points, and mark the side quarter points. On your T-shirt, match the center front and back points, and mark. Match those points to find and mark the quarter points (Figure 8).

4 With right sides together, pin the ribbing seam to the neckline at the center back point. The pins should be close to and parallel to the fold on the ribbing. Next, pin the ribbing and neckline together at the center front. Finally, match the quarter marks on the ribbing and neckline, and pin together (Figure 9). Note: The shoulder seams aren't always the quarter points.

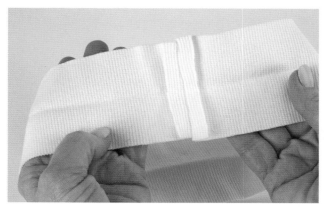

Figure 7

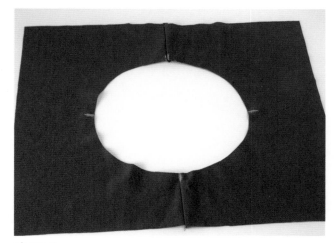

Figure 8

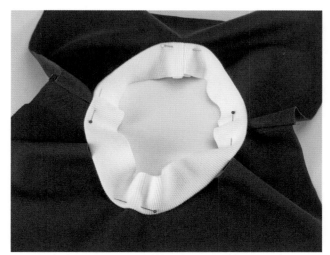

Figure 9

5 Stitch with the ribbing on top. Begin close to, but not on, the seam at the center back. Raise the presser foot and needle. Turn the handwheel to position the needle down in the fabric; remove the first pin. Lower the presser foot.

6 Gently stretch the ribbing to match the length of the neckline to the second pin. Serge up to that pin and then stop. Stretch the ribbing to the third pin and stitch. Continue in this manner around the neckline. Refer to Figure 6 on page 48.

7 Overlap the first stitches with 2–3 stitches at the end.

8 Chain off. Using a double-eye needle, slide the thread tail under the stitches.

9 Press the seam allowance toward the shirt (Figure 10).

Figure 10

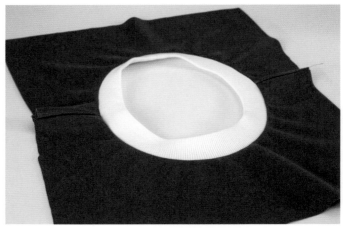

Finished Collar

Handy Tips & Techniques

Stretch the Ribbing

Stretch the ribbing only. If you stretch both the ribbing and the T-shirt edge, the neckline measurement won't be accurate, and it will gape when worn. Stitch at a moderate speed when applying ribbing to a neckline. You'll have better control as you stitch around a curve and, in turn, you'll be happy with the beautiful finished product!

Use stay tape to stabilize the shoulder seams.

Secure the Seam

There are two great methods for securing a seam: the fast method and the neat method. Both work equally well for different applications. The fast method is great when the stitching will be concealed (inside a pillow or a lined tote bag). The neat method takes an extra minute but is my preference when the stitching will be visible (an unlined jacket or top, or a decorative exposed edge).

The Fast Method

Chain off the edge for a ½" (1.3cm). Stop and raise the presser foot.

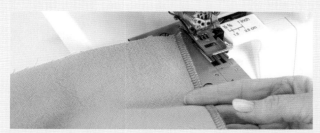

Bring the fabric around in front of the needles.

Lower the foot and stitch over the last 1" (2.5cm) of the seam.

Angle the fabric away from the needles and chain off. Clip the threads. There will be a small chain loop at the fabric edge.

The Neat Method

Stitch off the fabric edge for a couple of inches (centimeters). Clip the thread chain.

Slide a double-eye needle through your stitches, leaving the eye exposed.

Thread the serger chain through the eye of the needle and slide it under the last 1" (2.5cm) of stitches.

Slide the needle out from under the stitches and clip the chain tail. Apply a dot of seam sealant, if desired.

INSIDE AND OUTSIDE CURVES: MACHINE SETUP

Both inside and outside curves can be stitched with a 4-thread, 3-thread wide or 3-thread narrow overlock, depending on the application.

Inside Curves: Straighten Without Stretching!

Stitching curves on a sewing machine is easy. Maintaining the curve as the fabric advances under the foot helps produce a smooth arc. On a serger, when the knife is engaged, it's impossible to keep the fabric edge curved as it's overlocked. The knife will cut through it. To sew a curve, gently guide the fabric to the left of the knife and straighten the edge without stretching it (Figure 11). The knife should skim off the whiskers as it feeds along (Figure 12). If an arc is steep, stop frequently, raise the presser foot and allow the fabric to relax (Figure 13). Pivot the fabric if necessary. Repeat this method and complete the curve.

Stitch at a slow to moderate speed to develop good control of the fabric and machine. Knit and woven fabrics need the same gentle touch while serging curves. A curve on the most stable woven fabric will be on the true straight of grain for just a tiny fraction of an inch. Most of the curve is stitched on a less stable grain line, and any pulling on the fabric could result in a wavy edge.

Figure 11

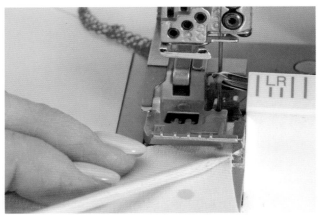

Figure 12

Handy Tips & Techniques

Adjust the Presser Foot

standard foot

specialty foot

If your machine has the capability, lighten the presser foot pressure one notch. Some sergers have an accessory foot designed for stitching curves. It's shorter than a standard foot and makes manipulating the fabric easier.

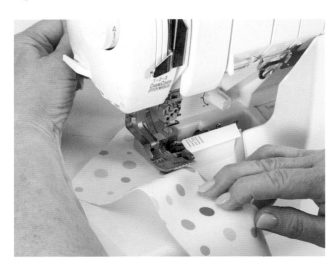

Figure 13

Outside Curves

Engage the knife when stitching outside curves. The trick to preventing the loops from hanging off the fabric edge is to keep moving the fabric to the right as it feeds along. The arc of the curve should stay in contact with the knife, allowing it to skim off the whiskers. Shorten the stitch length and stitch at a moderate speed for uniform thread coverage. Raise the presser foot intermittently to adjust the fabric position if necessary. Lower the foot and complete the curve.

Guide the thread tail through the stitching on the wrong side with a double-eye needle or large-eye upholstery needle. For an exposed edge stitched with thick decorative threads, clip the thread chain leaving a 3" (7.6cm) tail. Unravel the chain's stitches up to the fabric edge and tie the threads in a knot. Apply a dab of seam sealant. Let it dry and bury the thread tails between two fabric layers or under the stitches on a single fabric layer.

Outside Circle

You'll use the same technique to serge around the outside of a circle as you would for an outside curve with one difference:

Before stitching, clip a 1" (2.5cm) long notch in the fabric edge to create a starting point. The notch should be slightly shallower than the width of the stitch. When you reach the starting point again, follow the steps below for a perfect ending.

1 As you are approaching the first stitches with the your final stitches, with the needles and foot still down, pause and clip the starting thread tails.

2 Overlap 1" (2.5cm) of the first stitches with the final stitches and chain off (Figure 14). Take your time and keep the needle aligned with the first stitches.

3 Gently pick out the last stitches until just 2 or 3 stitches cover the first ones (Figure 15).

4 Tie off the thread tails, and dot with seam sealant. Bury the tails between fabric layers or under the stitching if just one layer of fabric was used (Figure 16). Clip the excess thread tail length (Figure 17).

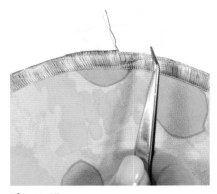

Figure 14

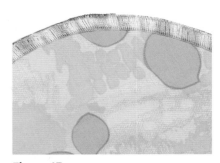

Figure 15

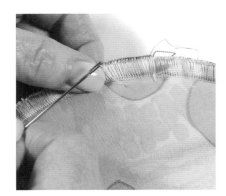

Figure 16

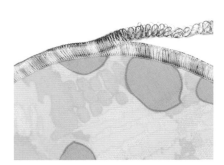

Figure 17

INSIDE CORNERS: MACHINE SETUP

Depending on the application, this technique can be done with a 4-thread, 3-thread wide or 3-thread narrow stitch.

The method for overlocking inside corners is very similar to inside curves. To prevent the knife from cutting into the horizontal leg of the L, the corner must be changed from a 90° angle to a straight edge.

1 Make a small clip (shallower than the width of the stitch) diagonally into the corner (Figure 18).

2 Begin serging, slowing down as you approach the corner (Figure 19). Gently straighten the corner without stretching it. A V-shaped gap will open. You'll notice that a fold in the fabric forms to the left of the foot (Figure 20). Smooth the fabric. You don't want to stitch a pleat in it. It will probably form a crease, but that can be pressed out.

3 Serge right over the gap and finish the edge (Figure 21). Press the fabric with its original angle.

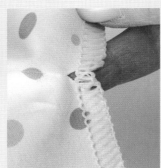

Handy Tips & Techniques

Inside Corners

Don't over straighten the second edge. If it's pulled too far left, the loops will hang off the edge.

Figure 18

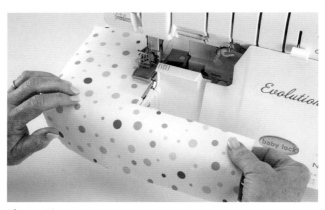

Figure 19

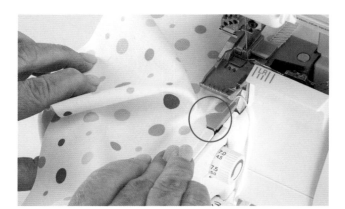

Figure 20

Figure 21

CONTINUOUS STITCH OUTSIDE CORNERS: MACHINE SETUP

Presser foot: Standard
Left needle tension: Normal or Right needle tension: Normal
Upper looper tension: Normal
Lower looper tension: Normal
Stitch length: Variable 2.0–3.0
Differential feed: Variable depending on fabric type (test on knit fabric)
Stitch finger: Engaged
Knife: Engaged

Depending on the application, this technique can be done with a 3-thread wide or 3-thread narrow overlock stitch.

This is a wonderful technique to master for exposed decorative edges on placemats, table runners or any project where the stitched edge is a decorative element of the overall design. It takes some practice, but beautiful corners are a great reward. The only thread tail to bury is the one in the final corner.

1️⃣ Precut your fabric to the desired finished measurements. You'll skim off the whiskers on all 4 sides.

2️⃣ Stitch the first side. As you approach the corner, slow down and stitch 1 stitch past the end of the fabric.

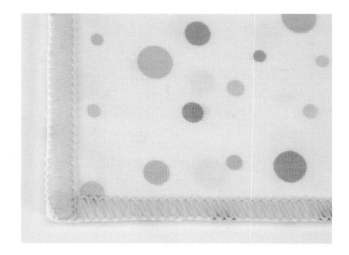

3️⃣ Raise the foot and the needle. Gently ease the stitches off the stitch finger by pulling the fabric back just a bit (Figure 22). You'll feel a little "pop." Don't pull too hard—be gentle.

4️⃣ Pivot the fabric and reposition the top edge under the needles (Figure 23).

5️⃣ There may be a little slack in the needle and looper threads. With the presser foot still raised, pull back the looper threads to just above the tension disks. Lower the foot and repeat the process for the remaining sides (Figure 24).

Figure 22

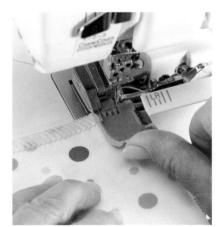

Figure 23

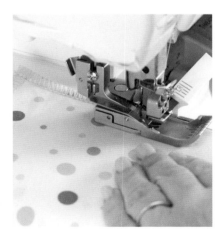

Figure 24

Also pictured: Wire-Edged Ribbon (see page 66)

Decorative-Edge Basket Liner

HERE'S AN EASY, ELEGANT HOSTESS GIFT for dinner at a friend's home. Purchase a basket and cover your favorite bread, jams or other goodies with this pretty liner.

 MACHINE SETUP

Decorative 3-Thread Narrow or Wide Overlock

Presser foot: Standard

Right or Left needle tension: Normal (match thread color to decorative threads)

Upper looper tension: Normal (decorative thread)

Lower looper tension: Normal (decorative thread)

Stitch length: Variable 1.5–2.5 depending on thread type

Differential feed: 1.0

Stitch finger: Engaged

Knife: Engaged

 MATERIALS

2 coordinating 18"–20" (45.7cm–50.8cm) squares of quilting cotton or linen

Thick decorative thread

Coordinating serger cone thread

Pins

1 On 2 layers of scrap fabric, test the stitch length with thick decorative threads. Find the length that provides good edge coverage without the stitches stacking on top of each other.

2 Pin the squares wrong sides together (Figure 1).

3 Hold the thread chain behind the foot until the needle takes 3–4 stitches in the fabric (Figure 2). Serge each edge, skimming off the whiskers as you stitch. Leave a 2" (5.1cm) thread tail on each corner. Hold onto the tail as you begin stitching the next edge (Figure 3). This helps keep a crisp 90° angle on the corners.

4 Finish the ends using a double-eye needle to bury the thread tails under the stitching (Figure 4).

Note: You can also use serger cone thread in the needle and both loopers. Using two different color looper threads is a fun way to highlight colors in print or solid fabrics. Shorten the stitch length when using serger cone thread. For a unique edge, try blending different thread colors together with a thread palette (see Handy Tips & Techniques: Thread Blending).

Figure 1

Figure 2

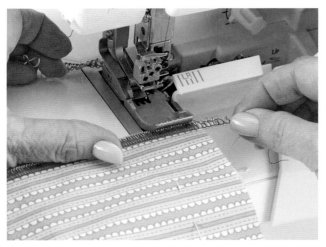

Figure 3

Figure 4

Thread Blending

Thread Palette

The Thread Palette is a platform with four pegs to use as spool pins. It holds up to four spools for threading through a single looper. Place the palette on the looper spool pin. Depending on your serger and the weight of your threads, you can blend up to four threads in one looper. It's particularly lovely when placed in the chain looper for cover stitching. Instead of the little blocks of solid color that stitching with variegated thread produces, thread blending subtly blends and changes the dominant color in the stitch according to how the threads twist as they feed through the machine.

Experiment on your serger with different numbers and weights of thread. A good rule of thumb is that the heavier the threads, the fewer should go through the looper. For instance, if I were using 12-weight decorative threads, I wouldn't use more than two spools in one looper. For embroidery- weight threads, I'd use up to four spools. It's a matter of testing and making samples to get just the right color combination, stitch length, etc. When using a wide 3-thread overlock for a decorative edge, generally two threads each in the upper and lower loopers work best (Figure 1).

If your serger feels like it's straining under the weight of multiple threads, remove at least one or change to a lighter-weight combination. Not all sergers can handle multiple threads in one looper. Do not put excess strain on your machine!

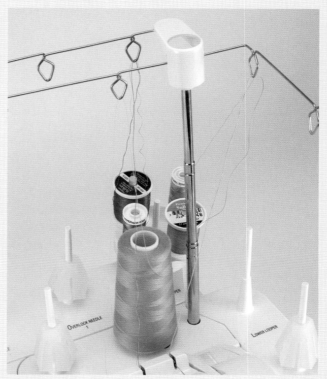

Figure 1

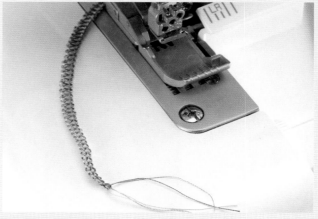

Thread-blended chain

3-Thread Rolled Hem Stitch

 MACHINE SETUP

Right needle: Normal tension setting; serger cone thread

Upper looper tension: 2–3 (Check the owner's manual.)

Lower looper tension: 5–7 (Check the owner's manual.)

Stitch length: Variable 0.5 –2.0

Differential feed: Variable

Stitch finger: Disengaged or down (For older models, you may have to change the throat plate for a rolled hem. Check your owner's manual)

Knife: Engaged

From one brand of serger to another, there are a variety of upper and lower looper tension settings for rolled hems. (Check your owner's manual for setting guidelines.) But no matter which make or model you own, the upper looper tension is usually slightly lower than normal, and the lower looper is set at a higher-than-normal number. Because the upper looper tension is loosened slightly and the lower looper tension is tightened significantly, the high tension of the lower looper thread pulls the upper looper thread to the underside of the fabric and the fabric edge rolls with it.

This is the narrowest stitch your serger will produce. The stitch is formed over a slender stitch pin instead of the wider stitch finger. A rolled hem is a very attractive edge finish for sheer and lightweight fabrics. It's useful for so many types of projects, whether you want to finish the edge of napkins or hem a chiffon skirt. Believe it or not, you can also make wire-edged ribbon, serge delicate pintucks, attach lace, and create ruffled, lettuce-leaf edging with this versatile stitch.

Right needle thread (right side)

Upper looper thread (right side)

Lower looper thread (wrong side)

ROLLED HEMS ON SHEER FABRIC

How many times have you tried to stitch a rolled hem on sheer fabric, only to have it fall off the edge once the fabric has advanced past the presser foot? There are several reasons this may happen. Sheer fabrics are woven with delicate fibers and fray easily. The needle pierces the fabric close to the raw edge, and the stitch has just a few fibers to hang onto. Therefore, it doesn't require much force to pull the stitch off the edge.

Fabric Handling

How you handle your fabric is very important for good results when hemming a sheer fabric like chiffon. Place your left hand flat on the fabric (to the left of the presser foot) and gently guide it along with your right hand (Figure 2). Never pull on the fabric from the front or back of the foot. As the fabric is feeding through, allow it to feed straight back. Pulling the fabric off to the left behind the foot (Figure 3) may cause the stitching to shear off the right edge.

Clip the Thread Tail

Chain off a few inches (several centimeters) and clip the thread tail with your scissors. Using the built-in cutter on the serger may inadvertently place stress on the last few inches (several centimeters) of the hem. Use seam sealant on the overlapping first and last stitches. Let it dry and clip the tail.

Use the Correct Thread

Use serger cone thread, all-purpose thread or embroidery thread on lightweight fabric. Don't use thick decorative thread. The fabric might not support it.

Adjust the Cutting Blade

Adjusting the cutting blade requires some testing, fine-tuning and patience. Move the cutting blade to the right slightly (1mm at a time) to trim off less fabric. The needle will take a deeper "bite" into more fibers as the fabric rolls under. The goal is to have enough fabric roll under for the stitch to be secure but not so much that the raw edge is peeking out from the stitches on the wrong side of the fabric.

Figure 2

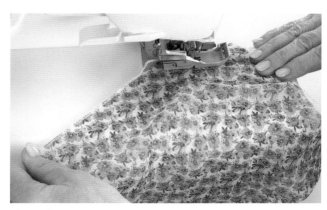

Figure 3

Stitch Length and Coverage

Another balancing act is stitch length and fabric edge coverage versus how many stitches the fabric can hang onto. A very satiny rolled edge is a beautiful hem treatment for firm fabrics such as linen and cotton, but the number of stitches per inch (2.5cm) required to create this finish may be too many for delicate chiffons and similar fabrics.

A very short (0.5mm) stitch length means that the needle will pierce and separate the fibers many times per inch (2.5cm). Spreading the fibers apart at such frequent intervals weakens the edge, often causing the stitch to shear off. What to do? Compromise, thread selection and test samples to the rescue! A hem (even on a miniskirt) is far enough from eye level to make it difficult to see the tiny bits of fabric between longer stitches. Lengthen the stitch little by little until the fabric can hold it securely. For fuller coverage using a longer stitch length, Woolly Nylon will fill in the fabric edge with the longer stitch length.

Rolled Hem Napkins

IT'S FAST AND INEXPENSIVE to make your own napkins. Cotton or linen fabrics are available in a wide variety of colors and prints, so you can customize your napkins for any occasion. Use contrasting or variegated thread for a pretty napkin edge.

 MACHINE SETUP

3-Thread Rolled Hem

Presser foot: Standard

Right needle tension: Normal

Upper looper tension: 2–3 (check the owner's manual)

Lower looper tension: 5–7 (check the owner's manual)

Stitch length: Variable 1.0–2.0

Differential feed: 1.0 or N*

Stitch finger: Disengaged

Knife: Engaged

* For a single layer of quilting weight cotton, if the edges draw in and pucker, lower the differential feed to 0.5. The front feed dogs are slowed down to hold the edge flat and smooth as it is stitched.

 MATERIALS

Quilting cotton or linen

Thick decorative thread*

Coordinating serger cone thread

Seam sealant (optional)

* Woolly Nylon and Woolly Nylon Extra are wonderful for napkin edges. The fluffy texture of the thread provides excellent coverage and is soft to the touch.

1. Preshrink your fabric. Cut 18" (45.7cm) squares, as many as you desire.

2. Serge each edge. Do not try to stitch continuously from one edge to the next. The corners will never look as perfect as when you start fresh on each edge. Hold the previous edge's thread tail as you begin the next edge for a 90° corner (Figure 1).

3. Apply seam sealant generously on both sides of all corners (Figure 2). Let them dry completely. Clip off all the thread tails (Figure 3). If making multiple napkins, serge all edges first, then go back and finish the corners.

Handy Tips & Techniques

Seam Sealant

If you've snipped too large an opening in the tip of the seam sealant squeeze bottle, you'll have difficulty controlling the flow, and you may end up with a stained corner. Instead use a cotton swab to apply the sealant to both sides of each corner.

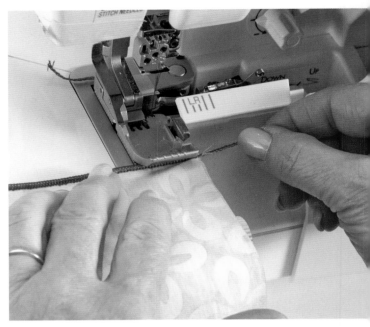

Figure 1

Figure 2

Figure 3

Serger Stubble

Serger stubble refers to those annoying tidbits of fabric that poke through rolled hem stitches. Will anyone notice them on a hem? Probably not. But if a rolled hem edge on a garment is closer to eye level, you want it to be perfect. Eliminate it by placing a strip of clear wash-away stabilizer (you'll need to see where you're stitching) over the edge of the fabric as you stitch (Figure 4).

1 Raise the needle and presser foot. Slide the stabilizer strip under the needle and lower the needle into the strip. This will anchor it.

2 Position the fabric under the stabilizer strip. Lower the foot and begin stitching.

The stabilizer prevents stretching as it encases the fabric edge for a clean, smooth finish. You'll love how perfectly each stitch lies on the fabric (Figure 5).

To remove the stabilizer, dampen the stitching with a wet makeup sponge and give the water a minute to dissolve the stabilizer. Support the stitches as you gently pull the stabilizer away. It's safer to pull it toward the body of the fabric rather than off the edge. To dissolve the stabilizer under the stitches, dampen a press cloth and press gently over the stitches.

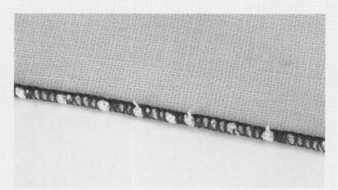

Serger stubble

stablizer strip

Figure 4

Figure 5

Wire-Edged Ribbon

DID YOU KNOW that you can make your own custom wire-edged ribbon on a serger? It's easier than you think. Create bows for wreaths, baskets and other items for special events, holidays or to match your home décor.

You can make your ribbon with one or two fabrics. Two coordinating fabrics placed wrong sides together make both sides of a bow very pretty. The upper looper thread is the most visible on a rolled hem. If you plan to use decorative thread, place it in the upper looper. Select matching color serger cone or all-purpose thread for the right needle and lower looper.

 MACHINE SETUP

3-Thread Rolled Hem

Presser foot: Standard, or check owner's manual for the suggested specialty foot*

Right needle tension: Normal

Upper looper tension: 2–3 (check the owner's manual)

Lower looper tension: 5–7 (check the owner's manual)

Stitch length: Variable 1.0 –2.0

Differential feed: 1.0 or N

Stitch finger: Disengaged

Knife: Engaged or disengaged

* Many sergers have an accessory foot with a hole or guide on the right side to feed the wire through. Check your owner's manual for your model's suggested foot. (They vary from one brand to another.) If you don't have a specialty foot, disengage the knife or move it as far right as possible. This will minimize or eliminate the chance of clipping the wire.

 MATERIALS

Fabric strips (1 or 2) cut to desired width and length*

26- or 28-gauge wire

Inexpensive craft scissors or wire cutters

Pins

Seam sealant

* Cut 2 fabric strips if you want your ribbon to be double-sided

Specialty wire foot

1 If using 2 fabric strips, pin them wrong sides together. Place the pins parallel to the long edges down the center of the fabric (Figure 1). Cut 2 lengths of wire, at least 12" (30.5cm) longer than your fabric strips.

2 Thread the wire through the guide on the foot. It's easier to remove the foot, position the wire, then snap it back on the serger (Figure 2). Pull enough wire to the back of the foot to hold onto as you stitch. If you don't have a special foot, raise the standard foot and slide the wire several inches (centimeters) behind the foot.

3 Turn the handwheel to lower the needle and lower the foot. Check to be sure that the wire is to the right of it. Hold

Figure 1

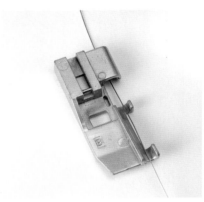

Figure 2

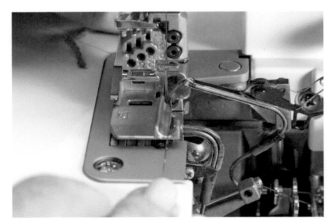

Figure 3

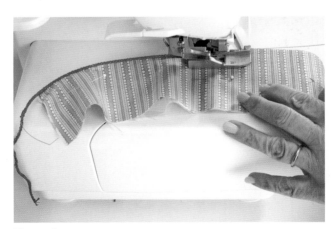

Figure 4

onto both the wire and the thread chain behind the foot and begin stitching onto the wire only. The slender wire needs help to advance (Figure 3).

4 Slide the fabric under the presser foot and stitch the fabric at a slow to moderate speed (Figure 4). Hold onto the wire as the needles begin stitching onto the fabric edge. The stitches will encase the wire as they roll the fabric edge. Keep an eye on the wire in front of the foot. If the knife is engaged, it could clip it.

5 Chain off and clip off the excess wire with craft scissors. Repeat the steps on the second fabric edge. Apply seam sealant to the clipped ends (Figure 5).

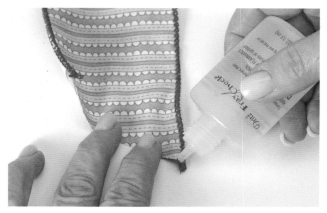

Figure 5

LETTUCE EDGE: MACHINE SETUP

Right needle: Normal tension setting; serger cone thread

Upper looper tension: 2–3 (check the owner's manual)

Lower looper tension: 5–7 (check the owner's manual)

Stitch length: Variable 0.5–1.5

Differential feed: 0.5

Stitch finger: Disengaged or down (You may have to change the throat plate for a rolled hem setup on your serger. Check the owner's manual.)

Knife: Engaged

This technique looks wonderful on light- to medium-weight knits and on the bias grainline of sheer woven fabrics. It's fluttery and fabulous on chiffon skirt and scarf edges. It's a fun edge on T-shirt sleeves and hems, knit shorts, capri pants and knit activewear.

To ruffle the edges of fabric, you'll do what you usually try to avoid: stretching the edge as you stitch. The lower differential feed setting will slow down the front feed dogs and hold the fabric back. But just the edge should stretch—not the body of the fabric.

Cut a sample piece of fabric to determine how much to stretch the edge. Let the needle take two or three stitches in the fabric and then begin pulling on the fabric from the front. If it needs help advancing, place your left hand gently in back of the foot to help it along (Figure 1). Pulling too hard from behind the foot may cause skipped stitches. It's a bit of a balancing act to stretch the edge just the right amount. Too much exertion will cause the stitches to pop off the edge. Too little pulling won't ruffle the edge. The short stitch length will help stretch the edge by crowding it with thread.

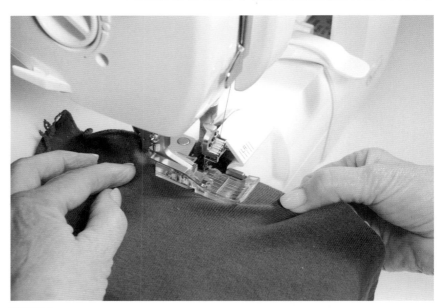

Figure 1

Handy Tips & Techniques

Use a Stretch Needle

If a universal needle doesn't produce a good stitch on your knit fabric, switch to a stretch needle.

Handy Tips & Techniques

Stretch the Edge

To prevent stretching the body of the fabric, keep your fingertips close to the stitched edge as you stretch it.

Pinch-and-Pull Method

If your edge is wavy but not ruffled, use the pinch-and-pull method. After the stitching is complete, pinch 2" (5.1cm) segments and pull the edge to increase ruffling.

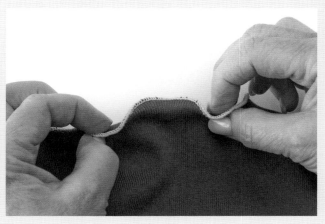

Decorative serger chains

Jacket with serger chain embellishments

Close-up of serger chain embellishments

DECORATIVE SERGER CHAINS: MACHINE SETUP

Right needle: Normal tension setting; serger cone thread
Upper looper tension: 2–3 (Check the owner's manual.)
Lower looper tension: 5–7 (Check the owner's manual.)
Stitch length: Variable
Differential feed: N/A
Stitch finger: Disengaged or down (You may have to change the throat plate for a rolled hem setup on your serger. Check the owner's manual.)
Knife: N/A

This is a thread-only technique—no fabric needed. Create custom trims for garments, quilts, home décor pieces, tote bags and purses. Thread your loopers with thick decorative threads for bold chains or lighter weight thread for finer

Handy Tips & Techniques

Which Stitch?

Use a 3-thread rolled hem setting for more rounded cording chains. Use a 3-thread narrow overlock stitch for a flatter chain. Your stitch length setting will vary depending on the weight of your thread(s) and the desired look.

3-thread rolled hem chain

3-thread narrow overlock chain

chains. Couch them to your project fabric using monofilament thread and a narrow zigzag stitch on your sewing machine. Braid three different color chains together for wide trim. You can weave them through knits as well as woven fabrics with my "Un-Beweavable" technique, too!

Place your choice of threads in the right needle and loopers (Figure 2). If using thick decorative threads in the upper and lower loopers, begin with a stitch length of 1.5. Lower the presser foot and chain off for approximately 8"–10" (20.3cm–25.4cm) (Figure 3). The stitches may be coiled (Figure 4). Press with steam and evaluate the appearance (Figure 5). Pressing will not only smooth out the stitches, but also elongate them. Adjust the stitch length as necessary until you're happy with the results. There is no right or wrong look.

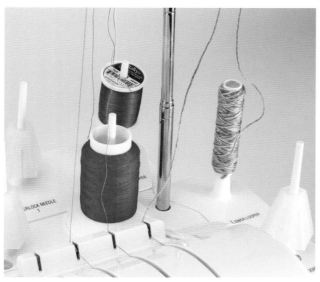

Figure 2

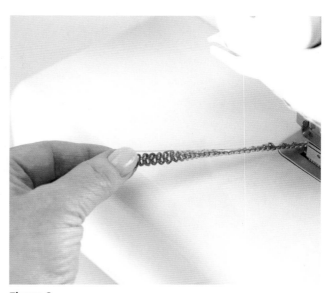

Figure 3

Figure 4

Figure 5

"Un-Beweavable" Ruffled Scarf

THIS SCARF IS EASY AND STYLISH. Select a T-shirt-weight knit fabric to make this great accessory for any outfit. Many knits are 60" (152.4cm) wide—a perfect scarf length. The ruffled lettuce edge adds a nice designer finish.

 MACHINE SETUP

3-Thread Rolled Hem

Presser foot: Standard

Right needle tension: Normal

Upper looper tension: Normal or slightly lower (check your owner's manual)

Lower looper tension: 5–7 (check your owner's manual)

Stitch length: Variable 1.0 –1.5

Differential feed: 0.5

Stitch finger: Disengaged

Knife: Engaged

 MATERIALS

¼ yard to ½ yard (0.2m–0.5m) T-shirt-weight knit fabric

3 cones matching or contrasting thread*

Double-eye needle for weaving

3 serger thread chains (or as many as you wish)**

Beads, charms, buttons or sew-on crystals for the ends of the chains

Edge Perfect Blade and 45mm rotary handle (for weaving perforations) (03) (This blade will fit any brand handle.)

Cutting mat

Hand-sewing needle

Seam sealant

* Woolly Nylon is an excellent choice for a lettuce edge. This fluffy thread covers the fabric edges fully, and the soft texture won't scratch or irritate the wearer's neck.

** See page 72 for tips on making serger chains. Experiment with different color combinations and decorative threads in the loopers. Chains should be 10"–12" (25.4cm–30.5cm) longer than the scarf.

1 Cut the scarf fabric to the desired width plus ½" (1.3cm). Cut the fabric on the crosswise grain from selvage to selvage. The crosswise direction has more stretch.

The scarf in the photos is 6" × 60" (15.2cm × 152.4cm). The width is not critical; choose a width that appeals to you.

2 Begin serging the edges of the scarf fabric with a lettuce edge. Take 3 or 4 stitches at the beginning of the fabric before pulling the edge. Use a consistent amount of tension for attractive ruffling. Stitch down both long edges (leave the short edges raw—they won't unravel) (Figure 1).

3 Place the scarf on a cutting mat (right- or wrong-side up). Roll the Edge Perfect Blade along the desired weaving routes. Don't cut too close to the stitching (Figure 2).

4 Thread a bodkin or double-eye needle with a serger chain and weave it in the desired intervals. The perforations are approximately ⅜" (1cm) apart. You can skip over multiple intervals or weave through all. If you don't like the weaving pattern, simply pull out the chain and start over in a new pattern (Figure 3).

5 Finish weaving all chains. Leave the serger chain tails hanging from the scarf's short edges.

6 Thread a hand needle and hand-sew beads, buttons, sew-on crystals or charms to the ends of the chains. Dot the ends of the chains with seam sealant and let dry.

Figure 1

Figure 2

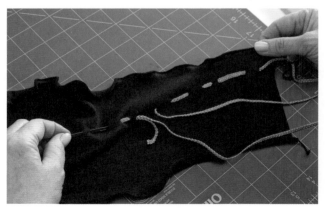
Figure 3

Handy Tips & Techniques

Test First!

Before working on your scarf, test your stitch length, thread and needle selection on scrap fabric. Practice ruffling the fabric along the edges. You'll determine the right amount of tension to exert when pulling. Pulling too hard will cause the stitches to pop off the edge.

If you want to slide beads onto your serger chains, be sure the serger chain will fit through the beads' holes before you buy them.

Stretch the Fabric

The perforations are almost invisible when the fabric is relaxed. If you are having trouble seeing them, give your fabric a tug.

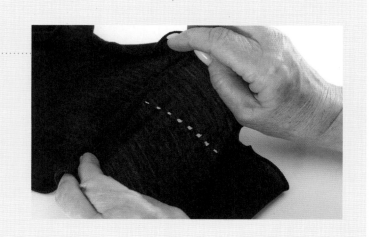

3-Thread Flatlock Stitch

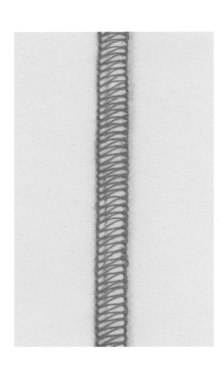

MACHINE SETUP

Presser foot: Standard

Right or left needle tension: 0

Upper looper tension: Higher than normal (check the owner's manual)

Lower looper tension: Higher than normal (check the owner's manual)

Stitch length: Variable 1.0–4.0

Differential feed: 1 or N

Stitch finger: Engaged

Knife: Engaged or disengaged*

* To prevent accidentally clipping the fabric, disengage the knife.

3-THREAD FLATLOCK

The flatlock stitch is a sturdy construction and decorative stitch similar to a 3-thread overlock—just a bit loopier on the edge. Because there is no needle tension, it can be pulled flat. It is stretchy, very strong and because the seam allowance is flat under the stitch, skin chafing is minimized. This is especially desirable for jogging pants and shorts as well as lingerie.

Handy Tips & Techniques

Use Tape!

Before threading the needle, set the needle tension to the highest number to close the tension disks completely. This usually prohibits the thread from sliding between the disks. If somehow the thread slides between the disks while stitching, place a piece of adhesive or painter's tape across the tension channel as a barrier. Rethread the needle with the thread over the tape. It works like a charm!

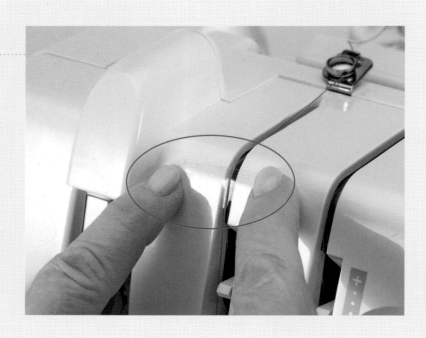

Fabrics are stitched wrong sides together for the looper threads to show on the right side.

For a wide flatlock, use the left overlock needle. For a narrow one, use the right overlock needle. Use decorative or contrasting serger thread in the loopers for easy embellishment and construction all in one step.

To flatlock within the fabric surface, use an erasable marker to mark the fold line. Finger-press a crease. To prevent clipping the fabric edge, move the knife as far to the right as possible or disengage it. Place the fold ⅛" (3mm) to the left of the knife (Figure 1) and stitch. Pull to flatten the fabric.

Figure 1

3-THREAD REVERSE FLATLOCK

The stitch is the same as the regular flatlock stitch, but the fabrics are stitched right sides together, causing the needle thread to show on the right side of the fabric. The needle thread forms straight "ladders"—perfect for weaving ribbons and trims.

For a wide reverse flatlock, use the left overlock needle. For a narrow one, use the right overlock needle. To create bold ladders, use a topstitch needle and thick decorative thread in the needle.

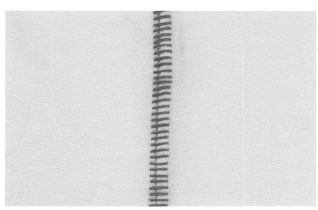

3-thread reverse flatlock

Handy Tips & Techniques

Help Stitches Lie Flat

If you can't pull the fabric flat after stitching, check to be sure there is no tension on the needle thread. Move the fabric edge or fold further to the left of the knife. (Your sample will help you determine the correct placement.) The loops will hang off the edge, but the stitch will pull flat.

2-Thread Flatlock Stitch

 MACHINE SETUP

Presser foot: Standard

Right or left needle tension: 0

Upper looper tension: N/A (use converter)

Lower looper tension: higher than normal (check the owner's manual)

Stitch length: Variable 1.0–4.0

Differential feed: 1.0 or N

Stitch finger: Engaged

Knife: Engaged or disengaged*

* To prevent accidently clipping a folded edge within the fabric surface, disengage the knife.

Figure 1

2-THREAD FLATLOCK

The 2-thread flatlock or reverse flatlock is slightly less bulky and pulls a bit flatter than a 3-thread flatlock stitch. It's best suited for knits but can be used on woven fabrics if there is no stress on seams. Try it on the Collage Pillow project on page 82.

Consult your owner's manual to see if your machine has 2-thread capability. If it does, you'll find an upper looper converter or subsidiary looper in your accessory kit (Figure 1). (Your machine's converter may look different than the one in the photo.) Follow the instructions for attaching it to your upper looper (Figure 2). The upper looper converter closes the eye of the looper, allowing a stitch to form with the needle and lower looper threads. The 2-thread flatlock and 2-thread reverse flatlock are stitched the same way as the 3-thread flatlock stitches.

Figure 2

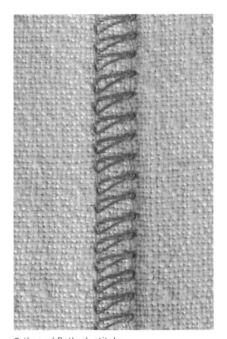

2-thread flatlock stitch

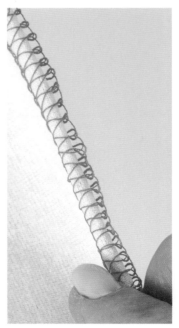

2-thread reverse flatlock stitch: Wrong side

2-thread reverse flatlock stitch: Right side

Ripping Out Serger Stitches

NOW THAT WE'VE TALKED ABOUT how to do a variety of stitches, let's talk about what we all dread having to do: Rip out serger stitches. Even when you've made your samples and fine-tuned all necessary adjustments, occasionally something goes wrong on a project and you have to redo the stitching.

What's the best way to remove serger stitches without overstressing or ruining your fabric? Use a sharp seam ripper to cut every third or fourth needle thread(s) (Figure 1) and pull the stitching out with tweezers. If you pull too long a segment of threads, you may damage and stretch the fabric. The looper threads will fall off the edge as the needle threads are removed.

Position the seam ripper point toward the edge of the fabric. It will prevent the point from accidentally tearing your fabric if your hand slips. Ripping out stitches is definitely time-consuming, but sometimes it can't be avoided. I like to think of using a seam ripper not as fixing a mistake but as holding myself to a higher standard. (It makes me feel much better about myself!)

Handy Tips & Techniques

Use a Lint Roller

Keep an adhesive lint roller in your sewing room. It's especially helpful to pick up all those little threads when ripping out stitches.

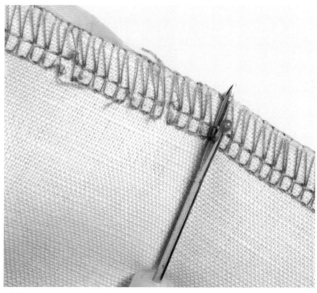

Figure 1

Collage Pillow

USE THOSE STASH FABRIC SCRAPS and jazz up your room décor with this Collage Pillow. I used three different denims and an indigo batik. If a fabric has two interesting sides, think about using both in your composition.

    The pieces of the pillow cover don't form straight edges. Some fabrics tend to fray easily when pulled flat under the stitching, and narrow points are especially fragile on narrow perimeter angles. To eliminate any loss of finished dimensions, the pieces are designed to be trued up after they are all joined.

MACHINE SETUP

3-Thread Reverse Flatlock (Pillow Front)
Presser foot: Standard

Right or left needle tension: 0 (decorative thread)

Upper looper tension: Higher than normal (check the owner's manual)

Lower looper tension: Higher than normal (check the owner's manual)

Stitch length: Variable 1.0–4.0

Differential feed: 1.0 or N

Stitch finger: Engaged

Knife: Engaged or disengaged

Note: You may also set up your machine for a 2-thread flatlock stitch. See instructions on page 82.

4-Thread Overlock (Assembling Front and Back)
Presser foot: Standard

Left needle tension: Normal

Right needle tension: Normal

Upper looper tension: Normal

Lower looper tension: Normal

Stitch length: Variable 2.5–3.5

Differential feed: Variable depending on fabric type (test lengthwise and crosswise on knit fabric)

Stitch finger: Engaged

Knife: Engaged

MATERIALS

3 to 4 fabrics

Fusible interfacing

Pattern pieces 1–6 (see pages 88–89)

Topstitch needle

Decorative thread (for needle)

2 matching threads (for loopers)

¼" (6mm) wide ribbon or fibers for weaving (if desired)

Bodkin or double-eye needle for weaving

4 cones matching thread

18" (46cm) pillow form

1 Using the pattern pieces provided, cut 1 of each piece (Figure 1). The pieces are numbered according to construction order. Don't worry about grainlines on these pieces. Position the pattern pieces as desired (or as they fit) on your fabrics.

2 Cut the following back pieces on the lengthwise, crosswise or bias grainlines:Cut (1) 10¾" × 18" (23.7cm × 45.7cm) of fabric and interfacing; Cut (1) 14⅜" × 18" (36.5cm × 45.7cm) of fabric and interfacing; Cut (1) 19" (48.3cm) square fusible interfacing (for pillow front).

3 Pin piece 1 to piece 2 (Figure 2). WIth a ⅜" (1cm) seam allowance, stitch the pieces together at a slow-to-moderate speed (Figure 3). The curve should be smooth. If necessary,

stop, raise the foot with the needles still in the fabric and adjust the fabric. After stitching each seam, pull the fabrics flat to expose the ladders and press flat (Figure 4).

4 Pin piece 3 in place and serge to join. Once again, pull the seam flat and press. Before joining piece 4, trim the inside edge of piece 3 even with piece 2 (Figure 5). Continue in this manner, joining the pieces in order and pressing the seams flat before adding the next piece. Press your pillow front when complete (Figure 6).

5 If desired, weave ribbons through the reverse flatlock ladders (Figure 7). To add visual complexity, try two different weaving patterns: over 3, under 2; over 2, under 3; or whatever pattern you prefer.

Figure 1

Figure 2

Figure 3

Figure 4

6 After weaving is complete, fuse interfacing to the wrong side of the pillow front according to the manufacturer's directions.

7 Trim the outside edges to an 18" (45.7cm) square (Figure 8). (A gridded cutting mat is very helpful.)

Trim this edge flat

Figure 5

Figure 6

Figure 7

Figure 8

8 Fuse interfacing to the wrong sides of each back piece. Press a 1⅜" (3.5cm) hem on one 18" (45.7cm) edge of each piece (Figure 9).

9 Create a blind hem fold as shown in Figure 10. Pin the fold in place with a ⅜" (1cm) lip of fabric to the right of the top fold.

10 Using the reverse flatlock stitch, stitch with the fold just to the left of the knife. The knife will trim away the ⅜" (1cm) lip of fabric (Figure 11). Pull the fabric flat and press (Figure 12).

11 Repeat steps 9 and 10 on the other back piece.

12 Place the larger back piece right-side up on your cutting mat. Position the smaller back piece right-side up on top of the larger one. They should overlap approximately 4¾" (12.1cm) and form an 18" (45.7cm) square (Figure 13). Adjust as necessary.

13 Use a sewing machine to baste the overlapped pieces together.

Figure 9

Figure 10

Figure 11

Figure 12

Figure 13

14 Set up your serger for a 4-thread overlock stitch. Pin the pillow front and back, right sides together (Figure 14).

15 Stitch the pieces together, allowing the knife to trim off ¼" (6mm) (Figure 15).

16 Secure the corners as described in Secure the Seam (page 51) or pull the thread tail under the last few stitches. (The Fast Method is great for inside corners.)

17 Turn the pillow cover right-side out and press the side seams. Stuff the pillow form inside the cover.

Figure 14

Figure 15

Finished pillow cover front

Finished pillow cover back

Pillow Templates
Shown at 35%; enlarge to 286%

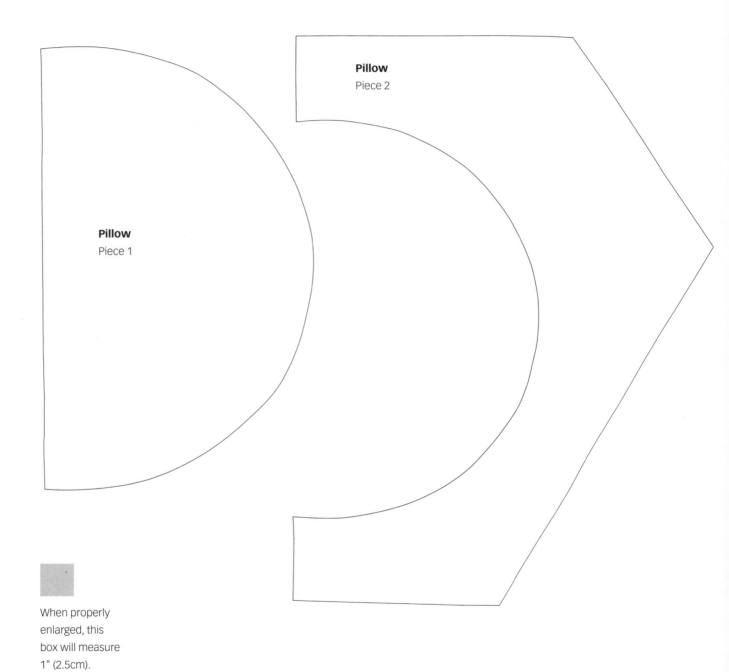

Pillow
Piece 2

Pillow
Piece 1

When properly
enlarged, this
box will measure
1" (2.5cm).

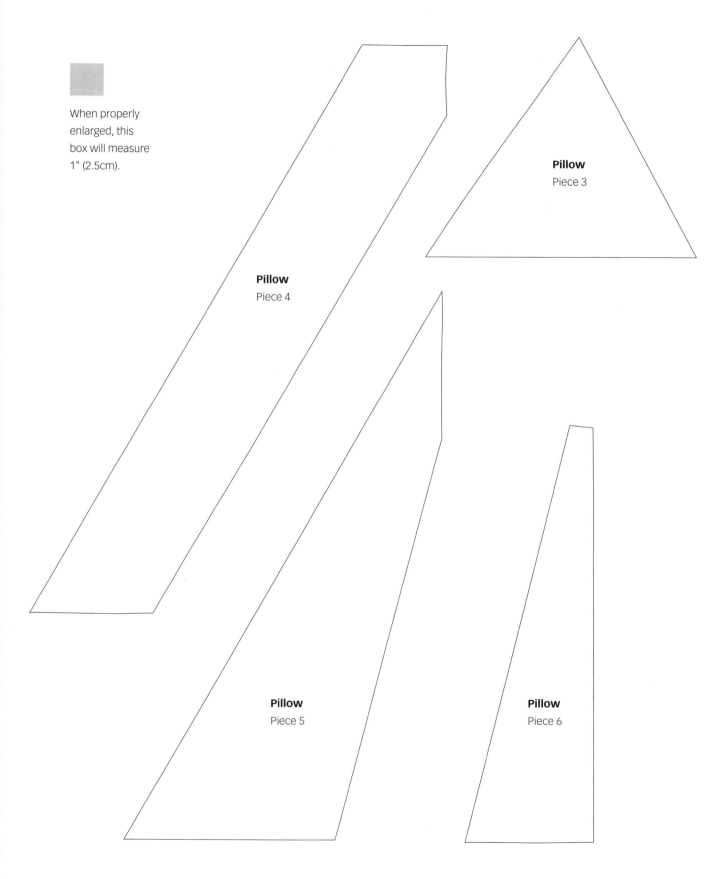

When properly enlarged, this box will measure 1" (2.5cm).

Pillow
Piece 3

Pillow
Piece 4

Pillow
Piece 5

Pillow
Piece 6

cover stitch

IN THIS SECTION, The cover stitch or cover hem is a versatile, attractive and strong stitch. Because of its high stretch capability, it's the ready-to-wear industry standard for hemming knit garments. If you have ready-to-wear T-shirts and activewear, the sleeves and bottom edges are probably hemmed with a narrow cover stitch. On the right side, it appears as two parallel lines of straight stitches. On the wrong side, the chain looper thread covers the raw edge.

Understanding the Cover Stitch
Machine Comparisons
Serger Conversion
Starting and Ending the Stitch
Pulling Out Stitches

Cover Stitches and Chain Stitches
Triple Cover Stitch
Wide Cover Stitch
Narrow Cover Stitch
Chain Stitch
5-Thread Industrial Stitch

Hems and Fabric Guides

Stitching in the Round
PROJECT: Embellished Jacket

Understanding the Cover Stitch

USING TWO OR THREE NEEDLES, the cover stitch appears as two or three parallel lines of straight stitching on the upper side of the fabric, and the chain looper forms loops on the lower side. Either side of the stitch can be used on the right side of your garment or project. Using the looper side of the stitch on the right side has become an important designer detail in activewear. It's a wonderful stitch for decorative applications as well. With serger or all-purpose thread in the needle(s) and decorative thread(s) in the chain looper, this utility stitch turns into a beautiful embellishment detail.

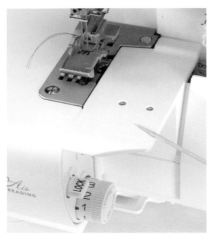
Cover hem table

Cover stitch needle position

Figure 1

MACHINE COMPARISONS

Your serger may have both overlock and cover stitch capability. If so, it will have five to eight thread positions. To convert from overlocking to cover stitching, some changeovers are required.

There are also dedicated cover/chain stitch machines with a chain looper only. These machines will have two or three needle postions, will not have upper and lower loopers or a knife and will not overlock edges. If you're happy with your 4-thread serger but want cover stitch capability, then a cover/chain stitch machine may be a perfect companion. A cover/chain stitch machine requires no conversion—so setup is fast. It's perfect for the sewist who frequently uses both overlocking and cover stitching.

SERGER CONVERSION

Follow the conversion instructions in your owner's manual. Most steps are similar from one brand to another. The upper looper and knife are disengaged, and the cover hem table will replace the overlock cover. The cover stitch needle positions are on the left side and slightly forward of the overlock needle positions.

THREADING

Threading the machine for a cover stitch is slightly different than threading it for overlocking. After threading the upper and lower loopers for overlocking, the threads are pulled under the presser foot. After threading the eye of a chain looper, an approximately 4" (10.2cm) thread tail remains under the machine bed before taking the first stitches (Figure 1). The needle thread(s) will pick up the chain looper thread as you begin to stitch.

STARTING AND ENDING THE STITCH

With the cover stitch, you must always begin stitching with fabric under the needles. You cannot chain onto the fabric. The machine will jam. The first few stitches will pull the chain looper thread to the top of the machine bed, but on some machines, it may take several stitches for the needle thread to catch the looper thread. How do you avoid missing stitches at the beginning of the fabric? Starter fabric!

Starter fabric can be any scrap of fabric from your project. Cut a piece at least 6" (15.2cm) long to check the stitch. Place it under the foot and needles. Turn the handwheel and lower the needles into the fabric. Then put the presser foot down! (Not lowering the presser foot is the most common error, especially when stitching thick fabric that occupies most of the space between the foot and feed dogs—even with the foot raised.)

Begin stitching and check the top and bottom sides of the stitch. If it looks like Figure 2, then the foot was not lowered. As you approach the end of the starter fabric, place your project fabric about 1mm from the starter fabric edge and begin stitching right onto it (Figure 3). Clip off the starter fabric once you've stitched onto your project fabric.

As you approach the end of the project fabric, align the same piece of starter fabric with your project fabric and stitch right onto it. Raise the presser foot and needles to the highest position. Pull the fabric straight back and clip the threads at the end of the finishing fabric. If your fabric doesn't pull easily, don't force it. Instead turn the hand wheel one full revolution away from you to the highest position. This will release the threads. The fabric should pull out from under the foot easily (Figure 4).

Finishing on scrap fabric allows you to raise the foot and release the fabric without losing any necessary stitches. For decorative stitching especially, it's difficult to add stitches and still have a perfect appearance.

Figure 2

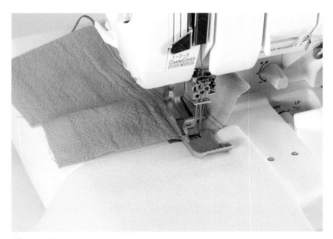

Figure 3

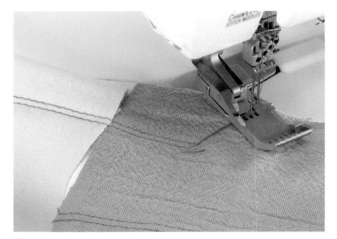

Figure 4

Figure 4

Figure 5

How to Remove the Finishing Fabric

Clipping the stitch between the two fabric pieces is fine if the final stitches will be encased in a seam. But if they won't be, here's a more secure finish: Gently pull out the stitches on your finishing fabric back to the last stitch on the project fabric (Figures 4 and 5). Tie off the thread tails, knot them together and dot with seam sealant.

Several serger models will chain off the fabric when cover stitching, but many will not. Check your owner's manual for this capability. For projects where the fabric remains flat, stitching onto a finishing fabric will prevent those last few stitches from unraveling at the end.

PULLING OUT STITCHES

One significant difference between cover and overlock stitches is that pulling out cover stitches is quick while ripping out overlock stitches is more time-consuming. The ease of pulling out cover stitches is a wonderful feature…but only if that's what you want to do. If you've had to shorten or lengthen some ready-to-wear garments, you can pull out the stitching in a few seconds if you catch the thread just right. The hems on ready-to-wear garments are sewn with a chain stitch.

To pull out cover/chain stitches, gently pull the chain looper thread from the last stitch to first. If after several inches (centimeters), the stitch "locks," pull out the needle thread(s) to that same point. Resume pulling the looper thread and repeat the process until all stitches are removed. You cannot remove cover/chain stitches from first to last. They are locked in this direction.

Handy Tips & Techniques

Clearing the Threads

How can you clear the residual threads from previous cover stitching to make room for another piece of fabric under the needles? It's simple. Raise the presser foot and while holding onto the thread tails, turn the hand wheel away from you until the threads pull straight back without resistance. Clip and remove stray thread tails.

Cover Stitches and Chain Stitch

YOUR MACHINE'S COVER STITCH may have two or three needle positions. Three needles will produce a triple cover stitch, and without the center needle, a wide cover stitch. With the center and right (or left) needles, or if your machine has just two needle positions, you can reproduce the look most often seen on ready-to-wear garments—a narrow cover stitch. A single needle produces the chain stitch.

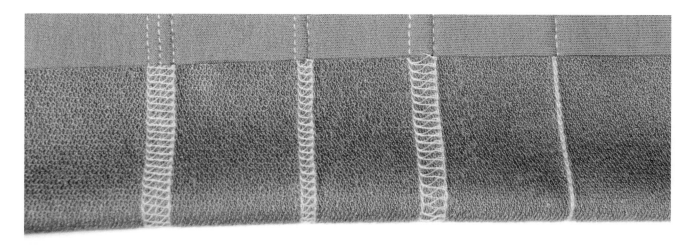

From left to right: Triple cover stitch, narrow cover stitch, wide cover stitch, chain stitch

Refer to your owner's manual for correct threading routes of the chain looper and needles as well as how to lock the upper looper. The upper and lower loopers are not used. And the knife is disengaged. All of the same instructions for stitch length and differential feed apply when cover or chain stitching.

 MACHINE SETUP:
TRIPLE COVER STITCH

Right, center and left needle tensions: Normal
Chain looper tension: Normal
Stitch length: Variable
Differential feed: Variable

 MACHINE SETUP:
WIDE COVER STITCH

Right and left needle tensions: Normal (no center needle)
Chain looper tension: Normal
Stitch length: Variable
Differential feed: Variable

Triple cover stitch needle position

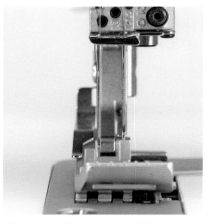

Wide cover stitch needle position

Narrow cover stitch needle position

Chain stitch needle position

Samples

The same principles apply to cover stitching as to overlocking: You may have to adjust the serger settings to find the stitch that works best for your project. Make samples and label them for reference later.

MACHINE SETUP: NARROW COVER STITCH

Center and right needles or center and left needles tensions: Normal (check your owner's manual or test for the better needle combination)

Chain looper tension: Normal

Stitch length: Variable

Differential feed: Variable

MACHINE SETUP: CHAIN STITCH

Single needle tension: Check your owner's manual or test for the best position

Chain looper tension: Check your owner's manual

Stitch length: Variable

Differential Feed: Variable

Note: The tension settings may vary from the cover stitch for a chain stitch. Check your owner's manual.

5-THREAD INDUSTRIAL STITCH

On many ready-to-wear garments, the seams are stitched with a 5-thread industrial stitch. A 3-thread overlock and chain stitch are serged simultaneously. The chain stitch appears approximately ⅛" (3mm) to the left of the 3-thread overlock stitch. Check your owner's manual to see if your machine has this capability.

Hems and Fabric Guides

STITCHING HEMS is one of the best utility applications of the cover stitch. But how do you know where the raw edge is if you can't see where it is from the right side of your fabric? Or what if your stitching is never straight? There's an easy solution—a fabric guide.

Fabric guide

WHAT IS A FABRIC GUIDE?

A fabric guide is a specialty attachment that is secured to the bed of the serger with guide fixing screws. It is most frequently used to cover stitch hems accurately. Ideally the chain looper stitches should cover the hem's raw edge. Because you can't see exactly where the raw edge is when the fabric's right side is face up, adjusting the fabric guide correctly will keep your fabric positioned correctly. The numbered lines on the fabric guide denote how far from the folded edge the stitching will be. Many hems on ready-to-wear T-shirts and other knit garments are approximately 1" (2.5cm) wide.

HOW DOES IT WORK?

Set up your serger for a narrow cover stitch. The photos show that the center and right needles are stitching the sample hem.

1 Loosely screw the fabric guide to the serger bed (Figure 1).

2 With the wrong side face up, place the fold of the hem against the vertical guide, or fence.

3 Slide the fabric guide right or left as needed to position the raw edge just to the right of the center needle. Tighten the screws (Figure 2).

4 Flip the fabric right-side up with the hem fold against the fence.

5 With the presser foot raised and the needles in the highest position, position the fabric under the needles and lower them into the fabric by turning the handwheel (Figure 3).

6 Lower the foot and begin stitching at a moderate speed. Keep the fold of the hem riding along the guide and complete the hem. Your stitching will be uniformly even from start to finish.

Handy Tips & Techniques

No Fabric Guide? No Problem!

A pad of sticky notes is a great substitute! It's sticky enough to adhere to the serger bed, but won't leave residue. Use the top edge of the pad as the guide and position it following the above steps.

Another alternative is to use a piece of painter's tape. The drawback to this method is that it doesn't provide a vertical guide. You'll have to watch the fabric edge closely in relation to the edge of the tape to be sure it doesn't wander.

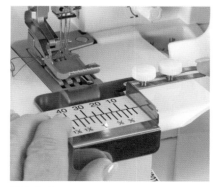

Figure 1

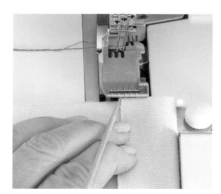

Figure 2

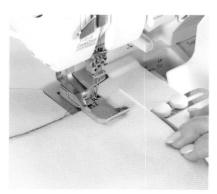

Figure 3

Stitching in the Round

THE MOST FREQUENTLY ASKED cover hem question in a workshop is the following: When hemming a T-shirt or any project in the round, how do I finish without accidentally pulling out the final 1½" (3.8cm) of stitches? The solution is simple!

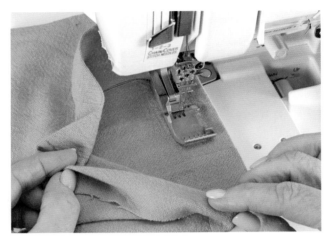

Figure 1

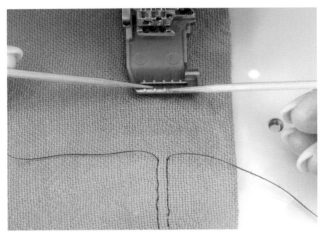

Figure 2

1 If you just threaded your machine, test your stitch and settings on starter fabric. This will also bring the chain looper thread up under the presser foot. If satisfied, raise the foot and remove the starter fabric.

2 Raise the presser foot and position your fabric under the needles (Figure 1). Lower the foot and begin stitching. As your final stitches are within several inches (centimeters) of the first ones, slow down. Using the indicator ridges as guides, be sure that the stitches are aligned (Figure 2).

3 Move the beginning thread tails to the right and left to prevent tangles. (It makes a neater finish.)

4 Overlap the first 2 stitches with the last 2 (Figure 3). Stop. Turn the handwheel toward you to raise the needles to the highest position and lift the presser foot.

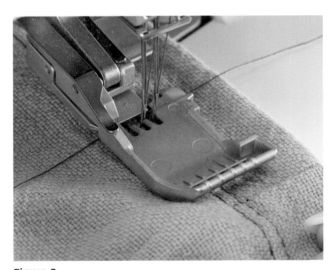

Figure 3

5 From behind the needle threads, with your tweezers or other narrow tool, (scissors, screwdriver), pull the thread ends forward 4" (10.2cm) in front of the presser foot and snip the ends (Figure 4).

6 With your left hand, firmly grasp the fabric behind the foot. Use a quick snapping action to pull it away from you. The needle threads will magically be pulled to the fabric's wrong side. This locks the stitches in place. Trim the threads on the wrong side (Figure 5).

7 There are still 2 threads on the fabric's right side (Figure 6). Those are the starting thread tails. You can clip them off—they're locked (Figure 7). Or with a hand needle, bury them between the fabric layers—my preference for neatness.

For more hemming tips, see the section on Knit Tips (page 108).

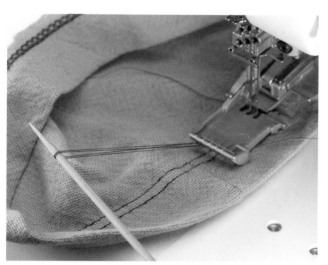

Figure 4

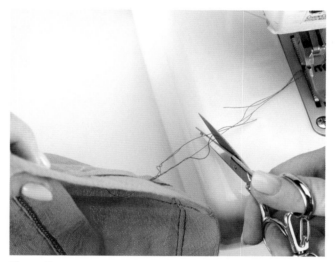

Figure 5

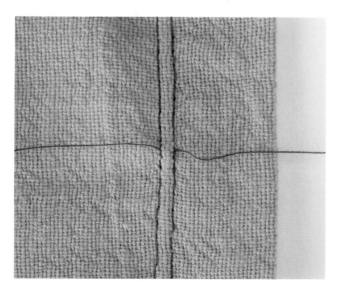

Figure 6

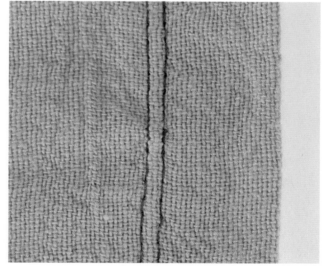

Figure 7

Embellished Jacket

USE THIS TECHNIQUE to create a beautifully embellished jacket. Make an exact replica of the jacket shown or come up with your own design. Have fun with it. Line placements are approximate. If your jacket is smaller or larger, spacing between lines may change. There is no right or wrong as long as it is aesthetically pleasing to you.

Select any jacket pattern with simple lines (no princess seams) for the best results. If your pattern has patch or welt pockets, eliminate them. They'll compete with the surface design. On-seam side pockets are a better option. The jacket featured in the photographs is my Top This! pattern. The fabric is medium-weight sweatshirt fleece—80 percent cotton and 20 percent polyester. Woven fabrics such as wool, cotton, linen, silk and blends can be embellished using the same techniques.

 MATERIALS

Jacket pattern*
Chalk, water marker or other removable
    marker
Decorative thread (see Handy Tips &
    Techniques)
Serger cone thread in coordinating color
Hot-fix embellishments
* See your specific jacket pattern for
    required fabric, thread, buttons and other
    materials. Patterns will vary. Select a
    pattern with simple lines and no princess
    seams for the best results. Cover stitch
    works best on knit or woven fabrics.

Handy Tips & Techniques

Decorative Threads

Experiment with different decorative threads to find one(s) that works well with your serger and fabric. Test to be sure the thread is colorfast (especially if you select red cotton thread).

For the best stitch appearance, your needle thread(s) should closely match the color of the decorative chain looper thread. Serger cone or all-purpose thread is recommended for the needle(s).

One decorative thread was used for all of the cover and chain stitching on this jacket. But you don't have to limit yourself. Use multiple weights and/or colors to add more design complexity. The decorative thread on the jacket shown is YLI Designer 6 100% rayon. It is no longer available. YLI Designer 7, YLI Jeans Stitch, Sulky 12- or 30-wt cotton thread, Madeira Decora and metallic embroidery threads are all great options. There are so many beautiful options available—too many to list.

Handy Tips & Techniques

Test Your Settings

Before you begin stitching the actual jacket pieces, stitch test samples. Be sure to purchase enough decorative thread and fabric to test all stitches and complete the jacket.

Experiment with different stitch lengths. Make notes on stitch length and tension settings for the chain stitch and cover stitches. Decorative threads vary widely in weight, thickness and texture. It's amazing how different a stitch looks with a 2.5mm or 4.0mm stitch length. The appearance will vary on different fabrics.

Test differential feed settings on the various fabric grainlines and record the settings.

1 If you plan to launder your jacket, prewash and dry the fabric prior to cutting the pattern pieces. Check laundering instructions on all hot-fix products if you plan to use them.

Cut out your jacket pieces following your pattern directions. It's easier to embellish the jacket pieces prior to construction. Most sergers don't have a wide space to the right of the needle, so the less fabric you have to manipulate, the better. If your pattern has darts, stitch them now.

2 Lay out the jacket pieces and draw on the embellishments with your removable marker or chalk. The lines are drawn on the wrong side of each piece (Figure 1). Use the figures on pages 105–107 to create a jacket like the one shown, or come up with your own pattern. The blue lines are stitched with a chain stitch and the red lines are stitched with a cover stitch. If you have multiple removable marker colors, draw the lines in different colors so you can easily recognize which line is which.

For alignment over unsewn seams, baste the pieces together and draw the line(s) across the seam. Pull out the basting stitches before stitching the cover or chain stitches. If you are drawing your own designs, avoid decorative stitching lines that cross buttonholes or other closure areas on the right front piece.

Figure 1

Handy Tips & Techniques

Perfect Alignment

Use those indicator ridges on the toe of your presser foot to stitch the embellishment lines exactly where you want them.

3 Set up your machine for a cover stitch using the settings from your test sample. With the fabric wrong-side up, cover stitch all of the red lines (Figure 2). Complete the cover stitching on every piece before moving on to the chain stitches. For tips on cover stitching the circle, see Handy Tips & Techniques: Stitching Around the Circle.

4 Set up the serger for a chain stitch following the settings from your sample stitching. Finish stitching the design with chain stitches (Figure 3).

5 If using hot-fix embellishments, add them to your jacket following the manufacturer's directions.

6 Construct your jacket following the pattern instructions. On unlined jackets, a 4-thread overlock stitch works well for strong seam construction.

Figure 2

Handy Tips & Techniques

Stitching Around the Circle

The most challenging part of the design is the circle on the upper left back piece. Because you are stitching a curve and aren't on the lengthwise or crosswise grainlines for more than a few stitches, some fabrics have a tendency to draw in toward the center. If the fabric "domes up" inside the circle, lower the differential feed setting to keep the fabric flat. Test the setting on scrap fabric.

If you're still having trouble, shorten the stitch length and work at a slow-to-moderate speed. Stop and lift the presser foot to pivot the fabric (very slightly) if necessary. Lighten the presser foot pressure for the circle. If your serger has a curve presser foot, use it. (The short length of a curve foot is similar to a sports car versus a bus turning a corner.) If you feel that a chain stitch looks better than your cover stitching results, use that instead. It's easier to maneuver around circles with a single needle.

Figure 3

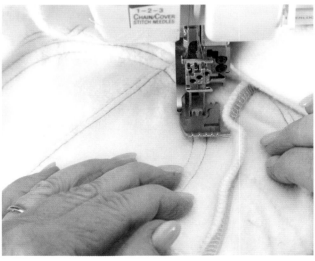

Cover stitching around the circle

Finished jacket front

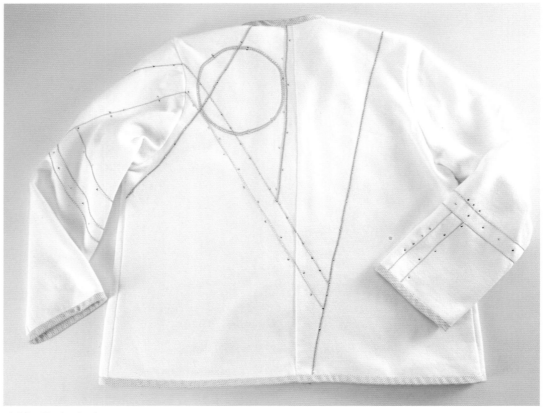

Finished jacket back

Embellishment Templates

Use these templates as a guide to embellish your jacket with the same design shown in the finished sample. Remember that all lines are drawn on the wrong side of the fabric.

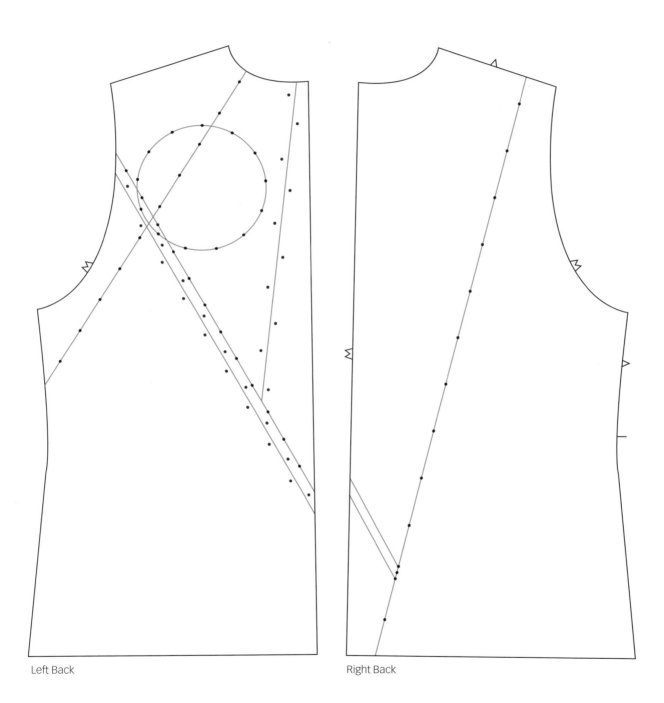

Left Back

Right Back

Embellishment Templates

Use these templates as a guide to embellish your jacket with the same design shown in the finished sample. Remember that all lines are drawn on the wrong side of the fabric. The parallel lines on the jacket front pieces alternate between ½"–¾" (1.3cm–1.9cm) apart.

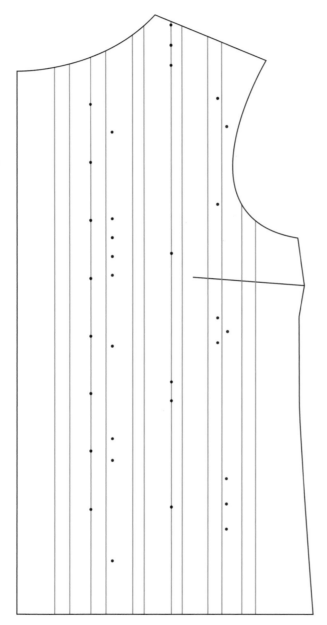

Left Front

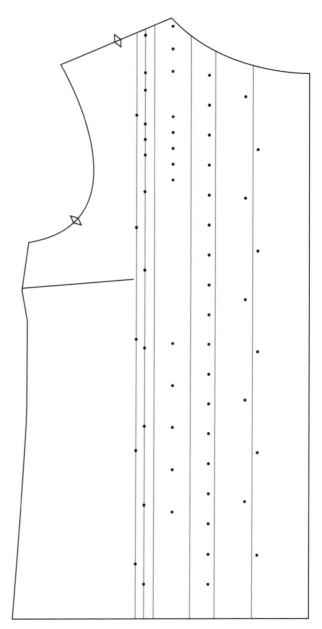

Right Front

Embellishment Templates

Use these templates as a guide to embellish your jacket with the same design shown in the finished sample. Remember that all lines are drawn on the wrong side of the fabric.

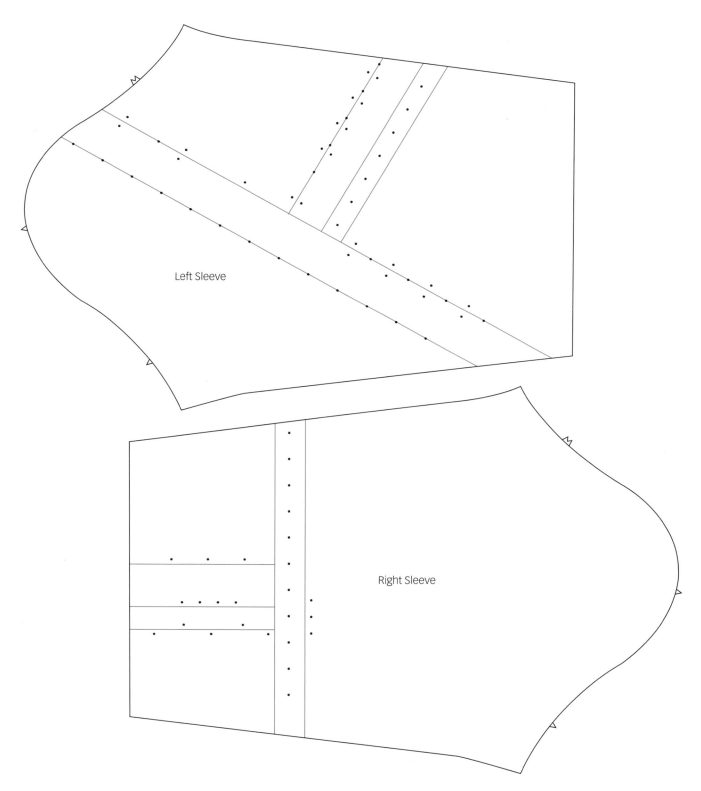

Left Sleeve

Right Sleeve

Knit Tips

THERE ARE SO MANY VARIETIES OF KNIT FABRICS available for sewists, this topic deserves its own section. Knit garments have become a wardrobe staple. Do you know anyone who doesn't own at least one T-shirt or knit jersey? Knits are comfortable, and many incorporate high-tech performance characteristics—especially in activewear and exercise tops and bottoms. Fabric weights, fibers and quality vary widely, and as with all other fabrics, testing on scrap fabric is the key to success.

As knits have evolved, the variety of fibers has grown. Many knit fabrics have become thinner, lighter and softer, and drape beautifully when worn. These characteristics that make them so luscious can also make them slightly more challenging to sew. Good news—there are wonderful newer products available to make using them easy! Let's look at a few products that will help produce professional results.

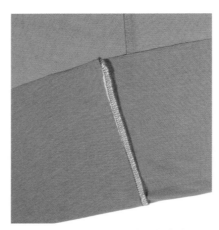

Lightweight rayon knit fabric with knit stay tape on one fabric edge

Right side of seam with knit stay tape: The seam is perfectly smooth

SEAM CONSTRUCTION

For most knit garment construction, a 3-thread wide or narrow overlock stitch is strong and secure with enough built-in stretch that you won't create popped stitches. A 3-thread flatlock stitch will also work well.

Recently I purchased a lightweight rayon knit fabric for a skirt. When testing my stitches on scrap fabric, I found that the fabric was difficult to control. What to do? Fusing a ½" (1.3cm) wide **knit stay tape** to one edge of the skirt panel provided just enough stability on the fabric edge to control it without making the seam rigid. The seam was perfectly smooth—even before pressing. There's no need to fuse stay tape to all edges; it will double the seam thickness.

Handy Tips & Techniques

Stabilize Armholes

Using knit stay tape in armhole seams will help stabilize the seam, making it easier to stitch, and it will also keep the armhole from stretching over time.

Wrong side of armhole stabilized with knit stay tape

DECORATIVE EDGE ON LIGHTWEIGHT KNITS

Instead of using binding on an unlined knit jacket or tunic, use a 3-thread wide overlock stitch and decorative threads in the upper and lower loopers to finish the jacket and sleeve edges. To add just enough stability, cut a ¼" (6mm) wide strip of **lightweight fusible interfacing** or cut the ½" (1.3cm) wide **knit stay tape** down to ¼" (6mm) wide and fuse along the raw edge on the wrong side (Figure 5). Thread the upper and lower loopers with decorative thread. Use coordinating color serger thread in the left overlock needle. Test the stitch length, etc., on scrap fabric. Stitch around the sleeve edges and perimeter of the jacket (Figure 6). The knit stay tape adds just enough body to the fabric edge to make stitching easy but won't change the hand of the fabric.

Figure 5

Jacket with 3-thread wide decorative edge

Figure 6

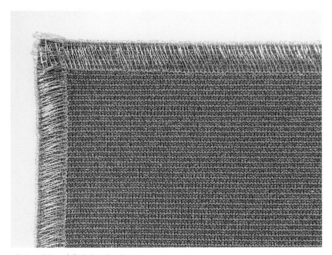

Right side of finished edge

Highlight Seams with Cover Stitch

A narrow or wide cover stitch is a beautiful choice to embellish seams, but sometimes getting perfect stitching on knit seams can be tricky. Here's a tip that not only helps produce beautiful cover stitching, but also strengthens the seams. (It works well on lightweight woven fabrics, too.) Test your machine settings on scrap fabric fused with knit stay tape. Experiment with different stitch lengths to get the desired effect.

Controlling a narrow double-layer seam allowance of an overlock seam under the presser foot can produce wobbly, uneven stitching. Try these tricks:

- Use a serger chain stitch or stitch the seams on your sewing machine.
- Trim the seam allowances to ¼" (6mm) wide and press open. Now your stitching surface is flat and easy to control.
- Fuse ½" (1.3cm) wide knit stay tape or cut ½" (1.3cm) wide strips of fusible knit interfacing. Center the tape over the seam allowances and fuse in place. Stay tape or interfacing strips add body and help control stretching while keeping the seams supple.
- Select a triple, wide or narrow cover stitch to highlight the seams.
- Stitch with the garment wrong side face up.
- Press with a press cloth.

This *Williamstown Skirt* was stitched with a narrow cover stitch, stitch length of 3.5. A thread palette uses 4 different embroidery threads in the chain looper. Coordinating threads were used in the right and center needles.

Right side of seam

Wrong side of seam

SECURING A HEM FOR COVER STITCHING

Adhesive web products have been available for many years. They are typically sold in ½" (1.3cm) wide or 1" (2.5cm) wide strips for hemming and work very well on stable "beefier" knits and woven fabrics. But the adhesive is sometimes too thick for the newer lightweight knits, and a stiff hem detracts from the garment's appearance. Fortunately, newer products have excellent holding power built into a very thin layer of adhesive. They won't change the hand of the fabric but will keep hems in place while cover stitching. (Most of the time, you can't even tell that it's between fabric layers.)

Using an adhesive web not only holds the hem more securely than pins, it may provide enough stability to eliminate accidentally stretching the hem as you serge. Hems generally go in the crosswise (stretchier) direction across sleeves and bottom edges. Again, testing will tell you if you need to adjust the differential feed.

The 1" (2.5cm) wide **double-sided fusible web** is my favorite for hemming T-shirts and other knit garments. If you prefer a narrower hem, use the ½" (1.3cm) wide strips. Before fusing to curved hems and necklines, cut clips through the paper and web at approximately 1" (2.5cm) intervals. The clips will allow the web to follow the curve.

The 1" (2.5cm) wide knit stay tape is perfect to keep hem edges from stretching out of shape from wear and laundering on very unstable knits. (Cut a crosswise strip of scrap fabric and gently tug on it. If it doesn't recover its original dimension, using knit stay tape will keep your garment looking better longer.) Fuse it to the raw edge before hemming. It will give the hem stability without losing flexibility.

Cover hem stitched with double-sided fusible web

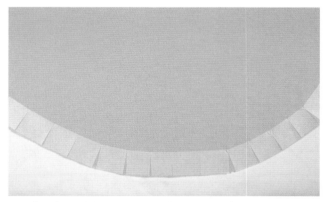

Cut clips through the paper web along a curved edge.

Handy Tips & Techniques

Extra Fabric

Purchase enough extra fabric to check all of your serger settings, thread, needle type and how to handle the fabric while serging. Operator technique is a critical element of success when working with knits.

APPLYING ADHESIVE WEB

Follow the manufacturer's directions for fusing the adhesive web to your fabric (Figure 1). Before peeling off the paper strip, use it to press up the 1" (2.5cm) hem (Figure 2). It's crisp enough to fold over. Once the hem is pressed, peel away the paper (Figure 3) and press the fabric layers together (Figure 4). Use a press cloth and an up-and-down motion with your iron. Sliding the iron back and forth can stretch the fabric (especially with steam).

Figure 1

Figure 2

Figure 3

Figure 4

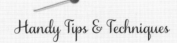

Handy Tips & Techniques

Stretching Knit Fabrics

When pressing with steam on knit fabric, it's easy to stretch the fabric. Use an up-and-down rather than sliding motion with the iron. The combination of the back-and-forth motion with steam can stretch the fabric.

Knit fabrics have a tendency to shine when pressed. A 100 percent cotton or silk organza press cloth will help prevent this.

Troubleshooting

HERE ARE SOME TIPS for pinpointing and solving problems. If your serger is still not working properly, have a factory-authorized technician check it.

SERGER MAINTENANCE

If your serger stitch isn't forming properly, don't panic. When was the last time it was cleaned and tuned up? All machines need proper maintenance to operate well. Routine home maintenance—vacuuming out the lint, oiling (if needed), using a dust cover when the machine isn't in use—will keep your serger in good running order.

THE MACHINE WON'T START

Is the plug secure in the machine and outlet? Is the power switch on? Some sergers won't start if the presser foot isn't lowered and the side and front covers aren't closed. If you have a looper air-threading system, is the lever in the serging position?

THE MACHINE IS RUNNING BUT NOT FORMING STITCHES

Are the loopers and needles threaded? Did you miss any thread guides? Check that the needles are fully inserted in the needle bar and in the correct position(s) for overlocking or cover stitch functions. Did you engage the upper looper converter/subsidiary looper for a 2-thread stitch?

MACHINE JAMS

Recheck for incorrect threading. Check for tangles or knots in thread. Is the thread caught under the cone or spool? If so, use a thread net or foam pad under the cone. The presser foot pressure may be too light and not advancing the fabric correctly. If the knife is disengaged, check that the fabric isn't too far to the right. It may be snagged on the upper looper. The stitch length may be too short for the fabric or thicker threads. If using thick specialty threads, hold onto the thread tail until the needles begin stitching in the fabric.

Cover/chain stitching: Stitching must be started with fabric under the needle(s). Some machines will chain off the fabric with a cover/chain stitch. Others will jam. Check your manual.

Use canned air and a mini vacuum hose to clean the lint out of your machine.

FABRIC WON'T FEED UNDER THE PRESSER FOOT

Lift the toe of the foot to help the feed dogs grab the fabric. For thick, lofty fabrics, raise the presser foot and slide the fabric underneath. Lengthen the stitch for heavier fabrics. Brush lint out of the feed dogs. Check to be sure the presser foot is lowered.

SKIPPED OR POORLY FORMED STITCHES

Check for correct threading and tension settings and that the antenna is fully extended. Is the presser foot down? The needles may be worn, bent or have a burr. Replace them with fresh needles. A clicking sound when stitching often indicates worn needles.

The needle size and type may not be correct for your fabric. Stretch needles work well on most knits but not on woven fabric. Universal or EL x 705 needles are often recommended for woven fabrics. If you are using a heavier thread in the needle, switch to a topstitch needle.

Check that each needle thread is in the correct guide above it. Each needle thread should be vertical and aligned with its needle.

Are you pulling your fabric from in front of the foot? Pulling too hard can prevent the fabric from feeding properly. Pulling the fabric in back of the foot with your left hand may cause skipped stitches.

Use good quality thread. Thread with slubs or other irregularities can cause poor stitch formation. If using a computerized serger, be sure the LCD screen shows the desired stitch setting.

Some fabric finishes can interfere with proper stitching. Your fabric may need to be prewashed to remove some of the surface finishing chemicals. A quick way to check is to test stitch on another fabric. If the stitching looks fine, then it may be the surface finish on your project fabric.

THREAD BREAKS

Check for correct threading. Follow your owner's manual instructions for the correct threading sequence. Incorrect threading is one of the most common reasons for thread breakage.

Use good quality thread. Inferior quality thread will be more susceptible to breakage. Check thread tension settings. If they are too high, thread may break.

Change the needle. Rarely, but sometimes, a new needle can have a burr in the eye that snags and breaks thread.

If you are switching from a 4-thread to a 3-thread or 2-thread stitch, remove the extra thread cone from the thread stand. Occasionally a thread tail left hanging freely can tangle with an adjacent thread and cause problems.

NEEDLE BREAKS

Check for correct needle insertion. Be sure it's fully inserted in the needle bar. Is it the correct size for your fabric? If the fabric is too heavy for the needle, it may bend or break. Pulling too hard on the fabric may cause the needle to bend and/or

break. If using a cover/chain stitch foot for overlocking, the needle will strike the foot and break.

FABRIC IS NOT CUTTING CLEANLY

If the blade is old and dull, replace it. Check the suggested cutting width for your stitch. If a pin nicked the blade, replace it. Follow the manual instructions for replacing the blade properly.

Stitch at a slower speed on thick, heavy or lofty fabrics. A moderate stitching speed will allow the knife to trim these fabrics cleanly.

PUCKERING SEAMS

The stitch length may be too long or short for your fabric. Always test the setting on scrap fabric first. Needle tensions may be too high. Adjust the presser foot pressure. Check the differential feed setting. If it's too high, it might be gathering the fabric.

LADDERS VISIBLE IN SEAMS

The needle tension may be too loose, especially on stiff fabric (denim, upholstery, etc.). Raise the tension setting. If ladders are still visible, reinforce the seam on your sewing machine.

CAN'T CLOSE THE MACHINE FRONT WITH THE COVER STITCH TABLE ATTACHED

Is the knife locked/disengaged? Is the upper looper locked in the down position?

COVER AND CHAIN STITCH FORMATION PROBLEMS

Are the needles in the cover/chain stitch positions? Are the threads in the correct thread channels and tension disks? Did you change the tension setting for a chain stitch? Recheck the threading route for the chain looper. Did you miss any thread guides?

STITCHES AND APPLICATIONS

5-thread industrial stitch

- Combination chain stitch and 3-thread overlock
- Often used in ready-to-wear garment construction and other applications where seam strength and stability is important.

4-thread overlock

- Both overlock needles, the upper and lower looper threads form this balanced stitch. The second row of needle stitches adds strength and durability to seams.
- This stitch has enough give and elasticity for knits and woven fabric seams.
- Can be used as a gathering stitch when the differential feed and needle tensions are raised.

3-thread overlock (wide or narrow)

- One needle (left for a wide overlock, right for a narrow overlock), the upper and lower looper threads form this balanced stitch.
- It's a good choice for seaming knit fabrics and applying ribbing to neck edges, sleeves and waistbands.
- Both the wide and narrow 3-thread overlock stitches are lovely for decorative exposed-edge finishes.
- The narrow 3-thread overlock is a good choice for finishing raw edges on woven fabric when a seam will be sewn on a sewing machine and pressed open. It's also great for lingerie construction. Raising the differential feed setting builds in a little extra stretch in knit fabric seams.

3-thread rolled hem

- This unbalanced stitch is formed with the right overlock needle, upper and lower looper threads. The upper looper tension is loosened slightly while the lower looper tension is tightened. The high lower looper thread tension pulls the upper looper thread over the fabric edge as it is rolled to the underside.
- It's a delicate hem finish on light- to medium-weight fabrics. It is not suitable for heavy or bulky fabrics.

2-thread rolled hem

- The right overlock needle and lower looper form a 2-thread rolled hem.
- This stitch is suitable for sheer, very lightweight fabrics such as chiffon and bridal veil edges, and requires an upper looper converter or subsidiary looper.

3-thread flatlock and reverse flatlock stitch (wide or narrow)

- This construction or decorative stitch is formed with the left overlock needle (wide) or right overlock needle (narrow), the upper and lower looper threads. The needle thread has no tension on it to allow the stitch to be pulled flat. Stitched with right sides together, the ladders show (reverse flatlock), and with wrong sides together, the loops show on the fabric right side (flatlock).
- This stitch is used for lingerie and activewear construction. Flat seam allowances reduce skin chafing.

5-thread industrial

4-thread overlock

3-thread wide overlock

2-thread flatlock and reverse stitch (wide or narrow)

- The upper looper thread is eliminated, and the upper looper converter or subsidiary looper closes the eye.
- It is used for hemming and lingerie construction as well as decorative applications.

Chain stitch

- This stitch is formed with one needle and the chain looper thread and can be stitched anywhere on a fabric's surface. It appears as a straight stitch on the upper fabric side and a chain on the lower fabric side. It has more stretch than a sewing machine straight stitch and can be used for construction when seam allowances are pressed open.
- Because it's easy to remove, it's a good choice for an alteration stitch.
- Sewn with the wrong side up and with specialty thread in the chain looper, it's a lovely embellishment stitch on all types of projects. Fabric must be placed under the needle to begin stitching.

Cover stitch (narrow, wide or triple)

- Formed with either two (narrow or wide) or three needle (triple) threads and the chain looper thread, these stitches have numerous construction and decorative applications, and can be stitched anywhere on a fabric's surface.
- It's perfect for hemming and topstitching knit garments due to its high stretch capability.
- Create exquisite embellishments with decorative thread in the looper. Fabric must be under the needle to begin stitching.

3-thread rolled hem

2-thread flatlock

Chain stitch

Cover stitch

MACHINE COMPONENTS

Feed dogs
- Two sets of teeth under the presser foot advance the fabric as it is stitched.
- Differential feed allows you to raise or lower the speed of the front feed dogs while the back feed dogs remain at a constant speed. Manipulate the settings to prevent stretching and to create lettuce-edge ruffling and gathering.

Presser foot
- When lowered on the fabric, the presser foot keeps the fabric in contact with the feed dogs to advance the fabric while stitching.
- Accessory presser feet are designed for a variety of specialty techniques. Cording, ruffling, elastic and lace applicator are just a few. See Specialty Serger Feet on page 118 for details.

Upper looper
- The upper looper thread forms the loops on the upper side of fabric as it overlocks.

Lower looper
- The lower looper thread forms the loops on the lower side of fabric as it overlocks.

Chain looper
- The chain looper thread forms the loops on the lower side as fabric is hemmed or with decorative stitching in the cover/chain stitch function.

Stitch finger
- Found to the right of the needles, along with needle position, the stitch finger helps adjust the stitch width. When disengaged, a narrower overlock or rolled hem stitch forms.

Upper looper converter (subsidiary looper)
- Closes the eye of the upper looper for 2-thread overlock stitches. They vary in design and may be attached to the upper looper. Your owner's manual will tell you whether your serger has this feature.

Knife
- The knife or cutting blade trims the fabric edge while overlocking. A knob or dial allows you to move it right to left for different stitch widths and to fine-tune the cutting width on lofty, thick or very sheer fabrics.
- It can also be disengaged for cover/chain stitching and overlocking.

Specialty Serger Feet

THE VARIETY OF SPECIALTY SERGER FEET AND ACCESSORIES has increased over time and will vary according to your serger's make and model. Check with your sewing machine dealer or on your brand's website to see which ones are available for your serger.

Remember, just because each foot has a specific name, does not mean it can only be used for that purpose. Many feet can multitask and are very useful for numerous techniques.

Ruffler Foot

Hints for Ruffles

Make a sample to determine the necessary fabric length for your ruffle and cut at least 12"–15" (30.5cm–38.1cm) extra. The amount of ruffling varies with fabrics.

Managing both fabrics takes a bit of practice. It's helpful to angle the top (flat) fabric slightly to the right of the foot as it feeds. Feed the bottom (ruffle) fabric straight.

For tighter gathering, gently pull back on the top fabric while stitching. See page 43 for a tutorial on using the ruffler foot.

MACHINE SETUP

4-thread overlock
Differential feed: 2.0
Stitch length: 4.0
Knife: Engaged
Fabrics are stitched right sides together.

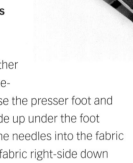

The ruffler foot allows you to gather or ruffle one fabric and simultaneously serge it to a flat fabric. Raise the presser foot and position the ruffle fabric right-side up under the foot (against the feed dogs). Lower the needles into the fabric to hold it in place. Insert the flat fabric right-side down in the slot over the separator platform. The platform separates this fabric from the increased differential feed setting of the feed dogs, thus keeping it flat while the bottom fabric ruffles.

The Elastic Foot

MACHINE SETUP

3- or 4-thread overlock; narrow or wide cover stitch
Differential feed: Variable
Stitch length: 4.0
Knife: Engaged or disengaged depending on stitch

Can you attach elastic using the standard presser foot? Yes. Will the gathering be consistent across the fabric? Probably not. It's difficult to maintain a uniform amount of tension when pulling elastic manually as it feeds under the presser foot. You may have tighter gathers in some areas and looser ones in others. A third hand would be very useful! The tension knob on top of the elastic foot is that third hand. Turning it clockwise will tighten the amount of tension on your elastic for more gathers. Looser tension (counterclockwise turn) will produce softer, looser gathers. The screw near the toe of the foot can be loosened to adjust the elastic guide right or left. Some elastic feet have indicator ridges on the toe to help you accurately position the elastic under the needles.

Before attaching the foot to your serger, insert the elastic. Place your index finger on top of the tension knob, and with your thumb, lift the toe of the foot to open it. Slide the elastic through the opening and over the roller. Pull at least 1"–2" (2.5cm–5.1cm) of the elastic to the back of the foot. Attach the foot to your serger. Turn the handwheel to lower the needles, and check their position on the elastic. Adjust the guide to the right or left if necessary.

How will I know how much to tighten the tension knob?

Elastics vary in the amount of stretch and recovery they have. Fabric weight will also affect gathering. Cut long strips of scrap project fabric for testing and adjusting. Begin with the tension knob adjusted to a moderate setting. Stitch 8"–10" (20.3cm–25.4cm) on your fabric strip. Stop and check it. If you want more gathering, tighten the tension knob, stitch another 8"–10" (20.3cm–25.4cm) and recheck. Repeat until you have the desired amount of gathers. Now you'll have perfect results on your project fabric.

Cording Foot

Handy Tips & Techniques

Choosing a Cording Foot

Cording feet come in several sizes that denote the width of the cording channel. Choose the one that most closely matches your cord width.

MACHINE SETUP (FOR CUSTOM PIPING)

3-thread wide overlock
Differential feed: 1.0 or N
Stitch length: 2.5–4.0
Stitch width: 4.5
Knife: Engaged

The channel on the bottom of this foot is a perfect groove for guiding cording as you make your own custom piping or insert purchased piping between two layers of fabric. Align the raw edges of piping and fabrics, and stitch with the fabrics' right sides together. For a professional zipper insertion, position the zipper teeth (right sides together on fabric) in the groove and eliminate the raw edges on home décor projects with zippers.

Beading Foot

MACHINE SETUP

3-thread rolled hem
Differential feed: 1 or N
Stitch length: 3.0 – 4.0
Knife: Engaged

Position prestrung pearls or beads in the channel on the right edge of the foot. Pull a couple of inches (centimeters) to the back of the foot. Place your fabric (right-side up) under the foot with ¼" (6mm) lip to be trimmed off by the knife. Lower the foot and needles. Hold onto the string for the first few stitches but don't pull. Stitch slowly. Lengthen or shorten the stitch if necessary.

Blind Hem Foot

Sample Perfect

Make a sample to position the guide perfectly. Fabric fiber content and weight will affect how the fabric folds and where the guide should be positioned.

 MACHINE SETUP

2- or 3-thread reverse flatlock
Differential feed: 1 or N
Stitch length: 3.0 – 4.0
Knife: Engaged

Press the hem allowance. With the fabric wrong-side up, flip the hem allowance under, leaving a generous ¼" (6mm) lip (raw edge) to the right of the fold. Pin in place. Position the fold next to the guide so the needle catches just a couple of threads on the fold. Adjust the guide and tighten the screw. Lower the foot and stitch. When finished, pull the stitches flat and press. See page 86 for a blind hem fold.

Pintuck Foot

Finding a Filler Cord

There are many filler options. Thick decorative thread, cording and yarn are just a few. Experiment to find the right one for your project. Stiff filler cords will change the drape of the fabric in that area.

 MACHINE SETUP

Narrow cover stitch
Differential feed: Variable
Stitch length: 2.0 – 3.5
Knife: Disengaged

Your serger pintuck foot will have a guide that is attached to the serger needle plate according to your instruction sheet. Draw the pintuck lines with an erasable marker on the right side of the fabric. Position the fabric so each line falls between the needles. Lower the foot, and stitch at a moderate speed. The guide will raise the fabric between the stitching lines.

Corded Pintucks
You may also have a guide for filler cord. Thread your cord through the guide hole and pull to the back of the foot. Follow the directions above for stitching. The filler cord will fill the space between the stitching lines, under the fabric.

Cover/Chain Stitch Foot

Tapes & Ribbons

The streamlined profile of this foot not only provides good control when turning tight corners and curves with differential feed, but the slot makes it perfect for attaching tapes and ribbons accurately.

This foot is designed exclusively for the cover/chain stitch needles. Its narrow width allows excellent visual access as well as the ability to stitch close to zipper teeth, piping, etc.

Curve Foot

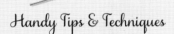
Small Pieces

While the short length of the curve foot makes it perfect for all types of curves, cover stitching small pieces such as cuffs and necklines on children's wear is so much easier with the curve foot!

The curve foot is approximately ½" (1.3cm) shorter than the standard foot. It can be used with overlock and cover stitch techniques. Because it's short, it doesn't cover both sets of feed dogs, eliminating differential feed. It's a perfect foot for turning circles and any tight arcs. A good analogy is turning a bus around a corner (standard foot) versus a sports car (curve foot).

Lace Applicator Foot

Choosing a Stitch for Lace

If you plan to edge stitch the seam allowance after attaching lace, a balanced narrow 3-thread overlock is the best choice. The fabric edge is flat and won't wobble under your sewing machine needle as a rolled hem edge might.

MACHINE SETUP

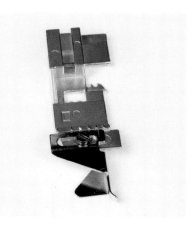

3-thread narrow overlock, 3-thread rolled hem or narrow reverse flatlock
Differential feed: Variable depending on fabric
Stitch length: 2.0–3.0
Knife: Engaged

Cut your lace several inches (centimeters) longer than the fabric to align with the needle.
Lace and fabric are stitched right sides together.

Stitching narrow strips of fabric, trims or lace to a base fabric can be tricky to manage. The lace applicator foot has an adjustable guide, like the elastic foot, that makes perfect results easy.

Align the lace header (the straight edge) with the right overlock needle. Lower the needle into the header to anchor it. Adjust the guide and tighten the screws. The right side of the lace should be face down. But if you can't tell which is the right side after examining it for 30 seconds, probably nobody else will be able to either!

Position your fabric (right-side up) under the foot with a ¼" (6mm) lip of fabric to the right of the foot. The knife will trim it off. Lower the foot and stitch in place. Press the seam allowance toward the fabric.

Index

THIS BOOK IS DEDICATED to everyone who loves and appreciates the creative process. Whether you sew for fun, for a living or as an art form, take some time to value the skills you've developed. But most of all, this book is dedicated to one of the most creative people I've ever met: my husband, Ira.

ACKNOWLEDGMENTS

My passion for sewing could not have grown without a very special place— Manchester Sewing Machine Center in Manchester, Connecticut. The late Aaron Cheerman, owner of MSMC for almost 40 years, was one of the most ethical, smart, kind and generous businessmen I've ever had the privilege to work with. He fostered an atmosphere of creativity for his staff and customer service was always his first priority. Wonderful friendships with Jennifer Stern-Hasemann, Pam Schneider and Pamela Leggett continue to be an added blessing in my life. I thank them for their expert advice and guidance on sewing (and many other things)!

Thank you to Rick Schiller and Melissa Kozuch for their friendships and assistance with ongoing serger and sewing projects. And I owe a huge debt of gratitude and admiration to Laurel Pepin and Alaina Tobin for their talents with photography, website management, workshop handouts and so many other skills.

Finally, thank you to Stephanie White, Amelia Johanson, Clare Finney and Christine Polomsky at F+W for their guidance and support while writing this book.

www.fwcommunity.com

19 18 17 16 15   5 4 3 2 1

Distributed in Canada by Fraser Direct
100 Armstrong Avenue
Georgetown, ON, Canada L7G 5S4
Tel: (905) 877-4411

Distributed in the U.K. and Europe by F&W MEDIA INTERNATIONAL
Brunel House, Newton Abbot, Devon, TQ12 4PU, England
Tel: (+44) 1626 323200; Fax: (+44) 1626 323319
Email: enquiries@fwmedia.com

Distributed in Australia by Capricorn Link
P.O. Box 704, S. Windsor NSW, 2756 Australia
Tel: (02) 4560 1600; Fax: (02) 4577 5288
Email: books@capricornlink.com.au

SRN: T5934
ISBN-13: 978-1-4402-4375-2

Edited by Stephanie White
Designed by Clare Finney
Production coordinated by Jennifer Bass
Photography by Christine Polomsky and Laurel Pepin

METRIC CONVERSION CHART

To convert	to	multiply by
Inches	Centimeters	2.54
Centimeters	Inches	0.4
Feet	Centimeters	30.5
Centimeters	Feet	0.03
Yards	Meters	0.9
Meters	Yards	1.1
Meters	Yards	1.1

ABOUT THE AUTHOR

In 1998, Gail began taking all types of classes at a local sewing machine center in Connecticut. Sewing quickly became a passion and a form of creative expression. Experimenting with all types of embellishment techniques is one of her favorite pastimes, and teaching classes and interacting with all levels of sewing enthusiasts continues to be a source of inspiration and fun. Gail especially enjoys encouraging sewists to love sergers as much as she does in hands-on workshops around the country.

She has presented classes and workshops at American Sewing Guild National Conferences and Chapters as well as at the following Expos: Original Sewing & Quilt Expos, Sewing & Stitchery Expo Puyallup, WA, American Sewing Expo Novi, MI. Her class, 40 Techniques Every Sewer Should Know, is one of Craftsy's bestsellers. Gail's articles have been published in *Threads* magazine, *Sew News* and Notions (ASG's quarterly newsletter). Her first book, *It's All About Embellishment!* is in its second printing and her DVD, *Cosmetic Serger-y* shows how to turn utility serger stitches into decorative techniques. She is a member of the American Sewing Guild Connecticut Chapter and moderated the Manchester Neighborhood Group for ten years.

Her studio and business, Gail Patrice Design (gailpatrice.com), are in Glastonbury, Connecticut, where she lives with her husband.

You've tackled your serger, now tackle your wardrobe!

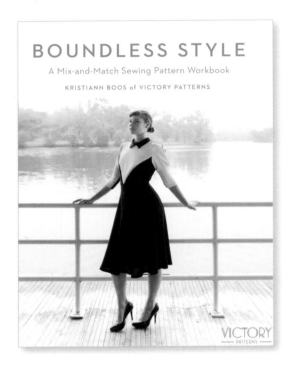

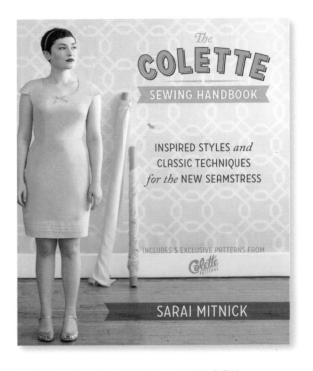

BOUNDLESS STYLE

A Mix-and-Match Sewing Pattern Workbook

KRISTIANN BOOS

Five bodices, five sleeves, five skirts—boundless style. In addition to helping you design your own clothes, author Kristiann guides you through all the essential sewing skills, such as installing an invisible zipper and balancing a hem. Every step is clearly detailed with photographs, illustrations and quality instructions. It's time to get sewing—your personalized adventure in style awaits!

THE COLETTE SEWING HANDBOOK

Inspired Styles and Classic Techniques
for the New Seamstress

SARAI MITNICK

Learn to sew beautifully by practicing the Five Fundamentals: a thoughtful plan; a precise pattern; a fantastic fit; a beautiful fabric; and a fine finish. Choose from any of the five projects—three dresses, one skirt and one blouse—in order to develop your skills, sew a lovely wardrobe and enjoy the results!

Watch *Serger Tips, Tricks and Troubleshooting*, an on demand web seminar, and get hands-on advice from author Gail Yellen!

VISIT WWW.INTERWEAVESTORE.COM FOR MORE DETAILS.